Seventh Annual Windsor Lectures

FREEDOM AND COMMUNICATIONS

University of Illinois Press, Urbana, 1961

FREEDOM AND

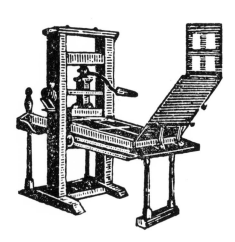

by Dan Lacy

COMMUNICATIONS

Foreword

The 1959 series, presented here, marks the end of the first decade of the Windsor Lectures in Librarianship. Since their inauguration in 1949, the lectures have become one of the most distinguished series in the country relating to books and libraries. In the intervening years, sixteen speakers, drawn from literary, academic, publishing, library and other fields, have participated in the program. All the lectures to date have been issued in handsome and appropriate formats by the University of Illinois Press.

The professional contributions of the man in whose honor the lectureship is named are outstanding. When Phineas Lawrence Windsor retired in 1940, he had rounded out a notable career of over forty years in librarianship, the last thirty-one of which were served as director of the Library and Library School of the University of Illinois. Under Professor Windsor's guidance, the Library School became internationally known as one of the leading centers for professional education. During the same period, the Library gained a position in the forefront of American university libraries. The endowed lectureship, created by several thousand alumni at the time of Professor Windsor's retirement, is both a recognition of his longtime leadership in the library world and fitting testimony of their loyalty, affection, and high esteem for him.

Dan Lacy, Windsor Lecturer for 1959, is eminently qualified to draw conclusions from the broad area of "Freedom and Communications" with which he deals in the present series. His career vi

has been varied. Since 1953 he has served as managing director of the American Book Publishers Council, the major trade association in the United States book field. Earlier assignments of importance held by Mr. Lacy included an instructorship in American history at the University of North Carolina, the assistant national directorship of the Historical Records Survey, the executive secretaryship of the National Resources Planning Board's Committee on Conservation of Cultural Resources, a term as assistant archivist of the United States, and another as deputy chief assistant librarian of the Library of Congress.

From 1951 to 1953, Mr. Lacy was assistant administrator of the International Information Administration of the U.S. Department of State and chief of the Information Center Service. His brilliant performance in this post won for him the Superior Service Medal of the Department of State, conferred in 1952.

As the former head of the U.S. Information Library Service at the time of the famous McCarthy investigations, Mr. Lacy defended the libraries from attack and was a leader in formulating two widely publicized statements adopted by the American Library Association and other organizations: "The Freedom to Read" and the "Overseas Library Statement." These eloquent documents played an important part in turning the tide of national sentiment against the hysteria for book purging and book burning which had seized the country. Mr. Lacy speaks and writes from first-hand experience, therefore, on "Freedom and Communications," and specifically on "what pattern of communications we need in this country to reinforce the preservation of freedom."

ROBERT B. DOWNS

*Director, Graduate School
of Library Science and
Dean of Library Administration
University of Illinois*

Preface

The place of the library as a part of the total communication system has been a subject of increasing concern to American librarianship. The purpose of these lectures is to sketch, in the broadest terms, a picture of the American communications system of the 1950's as a response to the almost overwhelming demands placed upon it by the rapid social changes of the period, to assess some of the deficiencies, and to suggest the outlines of public policy in the development of an adequate communications system.

To treat any one of these topics in detail would obviously be beyond the scope of so brief a work. I shall be more than content if it has been possible to set forth with some clarity certain theses: that our communications system must be viewed as a whole; that it now has an urgent—even a desperate—importance to us that is quite without precedent; that its inability to meet its present challenges exposes our society to serious dangers; and that the response of public policy to this situation must take the entire communications system into account. Such apparently disparate pieces of legislation as the Federal Library Services Act and possible changes in the pattern of the Federal Communications Commission's regulation of television are parts of the answer to a single great problem. Careful study of that problem as a whole is a major need, to which this preliminary essay can be no more than suggestive.

I am indebted to Dr. Robert B. Downs, dean of library administration at the University of Illinois, for the invitation to give viii

the lectures and for encouragement to deal with a subject rather outside the normal pattern of the series. I am particularly indebted to Robert W. Frase, associate managing director and staff economist of the American Book Publishers Council, and to Charles A. Siepmann, chairman of the Department of Communications in Education, New York University, both of whom have read the manuscript and made helpful suggestions. Many of the concepts that underlie the work have been developed in a long professional association with Mr. Frase. And finally, like all of us who work for the American Book Publishers Council, I owe a great deal to that rather remarkable organization for its constant encouragement to its staff to consider the problems of the book industry in their broadest relation to the public interest. The views here expressed are, however, my own, and not the Council's.

Contents

Chapter **I** *The Challenge*

For tens of millions of years man-like primates lived upon earth. Their life was not unchanging, and they were not without the ability to learn. But from the time the first of them used a stone to strike a blow until his distant descendant learned to shape a hand-ax, there dragged past endless ages that would have sufficed to re-enact dozens of times over the whole cycle of history from the pyramids to the atom bomb.

Somewhere in this timeless past, some of these naked, stone-using animals rose apart from their fellows and became men. Though we cannot date that event by strata of fossils or by radioactive carbon, in a sense we can say exactly when it was.

It was when they began to talk. With that event, timelessness was ended. Once man could symbolize reality, he could subdue it to his own mind. When the first word was spoken, the universe, in a quite literal sense, took on meaning, and the long course of human history opened ahead. The beginnings of speech were pregnant with all that man was to be.

But if men are human because they can talk, they are civilized because they can read. The words spoken face-to-face and retained only by memory were enough to teach the use of fire and tools and tame the cattle, clear the fields and plant the furrows, build the villages, pray to the gods. But there it stopped. Until there

1

2

were words that could be borne unchanging over great distances and to many men, and especially until there were words that could be preserved exactly and indisputably beyond the limits of memory, there could not be laws and courts and contracts and taxes and administration complex enough to organize a city or an empire. Nor could there be accumulated the organized bodies of knowledge that could support a civilization. This was possible only with the second revolution in communication, the invention of writing.

Writing had a dual effect. By making possible the accumulation and organization of a much larger body of knowledge, and its communication over longer spans of time and distance and with greatly reduced error, it opened the way to that much more complex organization of society that we call civilization. But it also had important consequences for the concentration of power within society. Even in a pre-literate culture there may be "mysteries" both of magic and of craft to which only a few are admitted, with a consequent exclusion of the remainder from the special power conferred by the secret knowledge. But this is not typical. Oral communication is essentially egalitarian. All normal men can speak and understand; and without writing, bodies of knowledge beyond common understanding are not easily built up. The skills conveyed by example and word-of-mouth—husbandry, fishing, simple agriculture, the building of huts—are widely, indeed almost universally, shared in primitive societies. Hence roughly equal participation in the economy extends widely through the group, as in the North American Indian tribes. Similarly, understanding of the issues requiring political decision is broadly shared and the rudimentary governments of primitive groups are likely to be essentially democratic in spirit.

Writing in its early uses, however, was not a means of general communication. Its use was to record and organize knowledge and to convey unique messages. It was a highly restricted instrument of large-scale public and business administration. In many ways its role in Sumer or ancient Egypt paralleled that of the electronic computer in our own society. The ability to write and to read was a technical skill of the upper servants of the court or temple quite analogous to, and as rare as, the ability to use an electronic computer today. Then, as now, enormous power was vested in the very much more complex and extensive bodies of knowledge that could be accumulated, stored, organized, recalled, and conveyed only by the use of the new communications medium. And that power was concentrated in the hands of those able to command the employment of this rare skill. Full participation in the economy and in the government could extend no farther than full participation in the power of writing. The extreme concentration of wealth and power in the ancient river empires corresponded to the exclusion of the mass of the population from access to the new communications techniques.

A very important change, even a "revolution," in communications can take place without necessarily being based on major changes in technology. All that may be required is a change in the social arrangements under which the technique of communication is employed. For example, though there were improvements in alphabets and in relatively inexpensive writing surfaces between Sumerian, Egyptian, and Babylonian periods on the one hand and the classic Greek and Roman period on the other, the techniques of communication were fundamentally unchanged. But a most important social change occurred. Literacy, from being a specialized skill of selected technicians, became a relatively widespread possession of the educated upper classes. Concomitantly, arrangements were set up to multiply copies of writings so as to serve this enlarged audience. Scriptoria, in which batteries of clerks wrote out copies of a work from dictation, were established and there emerged collections of manuscripts and even the beginnings of a book trade.

4

Only after this extension of its communications range could writing become the vehicle of a widely shared literature, or of a comprehensive body of science of history or other scholarship. The growth of culture in this sense was dependent on the emergence of a whole literate class and of means of duplicating writings in a sufficient quantity to reach throughout that class. Writing had to be extended from the letter or contract or account to embrace the treatise or the poem. At the same time the extension of access to written knowledge greatly broadened effective participation in the economic and political life of Greece and Rome in contrast to the autocracy of ancient Egypt. This was reflected not only in the city-state republics but even in the Roman Empire in which, regardless of the ostensible form of government, large bodies of aristocrats, technicians, and administrators shared in real power both in Rome and in the provinces. This "power elite," to use a contemporary phrase, was substantially defined by the range of access to the literate culture.

We see that each of these leaps—to humanity, to civilization, and to the high culture of the classic era—was accompanied by an equally radical transformation of the system of communication without which the cultural advance would not have been possible. The capacity of the ancient cultures to accumulate, to organize, and to convey knowledge and hence to master their environments was determined by the capacity and efficiency of their communications systems. And similarly, the range of participation in the communications system—in the ease of writing, how many copies could be made, how widely they could be distributed, and how many people of what kinds could get copies and read them— determined the range of effective participation in the economy and in the government. Egalitarianism in society was closely and necessarily linked with egalitarianism in communications.

In a history of continual subsequent change in the structure and complexity of societies and of their communications systems,

5

we can perhaps single out two other periods when the transformation was so swift as to be called a leap. One is the period of the Renaissance. If we no longer view this epoch as one of a dramatic rebirth of knowledge from ignorance, and if we attach less importance than before to the rise of classical humanism, nevertheless the radical economic and political transformations of the period cannot be obscured. They are in considerable part a matter of scale. The petty governmental units of feudalism gave way to national states, governing large populations under uniform bodies of law with the aid of professional bureaucracies and professional armed forces. The constricted medieval economy began its transformation into large-scale business enterprise of an essentially modern type. The machinery of banking and of international commerce spread from Italy over Northern Europe. Trading companies were developed which would shortly be able to sustain the exploration and settlement or conquest of new worlds. In almost every field of knowledge the bases of modern scientific inquiry were being laid. In all of its aspects, the society of Western Europe—hitherto so much smaller and less powerful than the societies of Asia—was accumulating the forces which in another century or two were to explode over the globe, discovering, exploring, and subduing both a new world and the ancient lands of Asia.

The accumulation of this vast potential involved the elaboration of major new bodies of knowledge, through the work of such men as Copernicus, Galileo, Torricelli, and Newton; the construction of complex systems of administration for both business and government; and the creation of a tremendously increased educated class to man this enlarged machinery. Such a series of developments would have been quite impossible within the limits of the communications system available to the Middle Ages. It became possible with the development of a printing industry, libraries, and a book trade. Within little more than

6

a half a century after the first European printing, substantially the whole corpus of Western knowledge had been reduced to print, thus multiplying its availability by a factor of several hundred. This is to say that within a couple of generations the number of people able realistically to participate in and make use of the new knowledge did not double or triple or quadruple but became *hundreds* of times as large. In this revolutionary increase in intellectual resources was generated the coiled power that was to impel Western European civilization from the margins of the Atlantic to mastery of the world in one brief epoch of history.

The second of these leaps came in the nineteenth century with the introduction of steam power to manufacturing and transportation, the political transformations that led toward modern democracy, and the institutionalization of science. The formation of scientific societies; the creation of university chairs of science and technology, as well as of history, linguistics, and other scholarly fields; and the development of canons of research all led to the creation of organized scholarly disciplines, on a professional basis, in such fields as chemistry, medicine, engineering, history, and philology and to a rapid and continuous increase in the quantity of knowledge making up those disciplines.

At the same time steam power made possible the factory system with its enormous increase in productivity. Perhaps even more important, rail and steamship transportation for the first time opened the way to a large-scale economy with a high degree of internal specialization. These two consequences of the new power sources completely transformed the economy of Western Europe and North America. One aspect of this transformation was that tens of millions of workers were drawn from agriculture and handicrafts, in which they employed skills handed down orally, and were set to tasks requiring at least a modest use of the new science and technology. By the latter half of the century the new science was indeed transforming the conduct of agriculture itself. At a higher level, the managerial class, required to have a relatively extensive mastery of the new knowledge, increased with equal rapidity.

At the same time, a series of revolutions was greatly broadening political participation. The American and French revolutions broke monarchical and oligarchical patterns and established a democratic theory of government. The Reform Bill in Great Britain and comparable gradualistic measures in Germany, Italy, and Scandinavia almost matched in results the more violent revolutions.

By the end of the century the advanced western countries had achieved a highly professionalized and institutionalized science, an industrial economy in which most workers participated in a science-based technology, and a democracy based on nearly universal male suffrage.

So vast an increase in the knowledge used by society; so radical a widening of the circle of sharers and users of that knowledge; and so intricate a multiplication of the complexity of social organization could not have been achieved with the handmade paper and the leisurely hand-operated printing presses of the eighteenth century. The literate class had earlier expanded many times over its tiny medieval size; but at the beginning of the political and industrial revolutions, it was still only a very small fragment of the population. Now it needed to embrace almost the entire citizenry, not only to provide the workers capable of acquiring new skills but also to provide voters able to exercise their new responsibilities.

The new technology of the age enabled it to respond effectively to the demands for vastly improved communication. In the industrialized countries this response took the following forms:

1. The acceptance of public responsibility for universal education through the level of literacy. This acceptance was general

8

by the mid-nineteenth century and the goal had been reasonably well achieved in America and Western Europe by the end of the century.

2. The application of steam power to printing, with a radical reduction in cost and an increase in the volume of print that raised it to a whole new order of magnitude.

3. The development of new, cheap methods of producing paper in limitless quantity.

4. The development of telegraphy, permitting an instant distribution of news.

5. The distribution of periodicals by rail. In the United States after 1879 this distribution was encouraged by a low uniform postal rate that made it as inexpensive to send a magazine from New York to San Francisco as from New York to Jersey City.

6. On the basis of the foregoing developments, the emergence of professional journalism and of highly organized industries for the publication and distribution of books, magazines, and newspapers. In 1800 there were about 40 magazines and 24 daily newspapers in the United States. None had more than a trivial circulation, running in most cases only to a few hundreds. It could hardly be said that any books were "published" in the sense that word came to have later in the century. By 1900, in contrast, there were 5,500 magazines and other periodicals and 2,190 newspapers, and their average circulation was incomparably larger. The book publishing industry by 1900 was able to issue and give national distribution to 5,400 titles a year.

7. The spread of systematic scholarly publication through learned journals and the proceedings of scientific societies. Typical in the United States were the *Journal of the American Medical Association,* initiated in 1883, the *American Anthropologist,* begun in 1896, and the *Engineers News Record,* published first in 1874.

8. The emergence of national library systems, both scholarly

and popular. The nineteenth century saw the development into their present patterns of the great national research libraries, like the British Museum, the Bibliothêque Nationale, and the Library of Congress, the birth of the research-centered university library, and the creation of the free public library system. The coincidence of the founding of the American Library Association in 1875 and of the Library Association of Great Britain in 1876 and the publication in the latter year of the pioneer report on public libraries by the Federal Commissioner of Education may be taken as marking the beginning of the modern library.

These eight developments, taken together, were far more revolutionary than the invention of printing itself. This is to say that the penetration of the written word throughout the social order increased much more dramatically in the century from 1800 to 1900 than in the century following the introduction of printing. Developments were as revolutionary in the accumulation and organization of learning as in its wide dissemination. The great research libraries that existed at the end of the nineteenth century simply had no parallel at its beginning. It is likewise noteworthy that the methods of cataloging and bibliographic control that still serve as the basic means of organizing knowledge in our society were also a product of the latter nineteenth century.

It is upon these radical developments in communication that the whole modern society in which we live is based. It is interesting to note that the societies that are only now attempting to industrialize and to stabilize democratic governments are having to go through the same revolution in communications. The attainment of universal literacy and the establishment of an effective publishing industry and adequate library systems, for example, are found to be among the necessary first steps in modernizing the economy of underdeveloped countries of Asia and the Middle East.

Public policy with respect to these extensions of communi-

10

cation has corresponded rather precisely to national objectives
with respect to industrialization and democratization. European
powers during the latter nineteenth and earlier twentieth centuries, for example, desired to modernize only those sectors of
the economy of their Asian possessions that directly served the
needs of the metropolis and preferred even in these sectors of
the economy to retain all important technical and managerial
positions in European hands. Nor was it desired to admit the
generality of the native population into political participation.
Only a very slight use of force was necessary to maintain this
exclusion from equal economic and political participation. All,
indeed, that was necessary was simply not to undertake to extend
literacy to the general population or to extend the communications system to embrace more than a very small and cooperative
elite. In contrast, tremendous efforts at mass education became
a first object of the new Asian governments after World War II.

Somewhat similarly, the Soviet Government, which was determined to achieve a swift and massive transfer of the Russian
population from a traditional peasant economy to active participation in modern industry and mechanical scientific agriculture,
adopted forced-draft measures to achieve universal literacy, large-
scale publishing, and widespread distribution of books, newspapers and magazines through sale and in libraries. In many ways
this movement paralleled the earlier communications revolution
in America.

But with a difference. The new Russian rulers wished to draw
the mass of the population into a modern economy, but to continue their exclusion from the government. Illiteracy and lack
of access to print had been an effective enough barrier to general
political participation in the days of the Tsars. Since this barrier
had been removed, however, and the population generally had
been admitted as recipients in the communications system, control had to be exercised at the point of input into the communi-

cations system. Only the government could print or broadcast, and for the relative freedom of literature in the Tsarist days was substituted the most rigorous censorship. (Parenthetically we may see an analogous phenomenon in the United States: the more unrestricted any means of communication in terms of recipients, the greater the social pressures toward control of input. One may say to his friend what he cannot speak from a platform, and from a platform what he cannot speak into a microphone; what may be played on Broadway cannot be filmed unaltered; and the book unchallenged in the university library may be attacked in the public library and banned from the newsstand. In all socially controlled—and that is, ultimately, all—systems of communications, the broader the outflow the narrower the input.)

I have thus summarily reviewed a series of social revolutions and their concommitant communications revolutions because I wish to assert that we are today passing through, or entering upon, another and yet more sweeping social revolution that will require drastic developments in our present system of communications if we are to preserve our freedoms. In the remainder of the present lecture I should like to suggest some of the characteristics of the contemporary social revolution that have especially important implications for communications. In the second I should like to examine our present communications system in terms of its response to the new demands. And in the third I should like to consider the adequacy of that response and undertake to draw certain inferences as to public policy in the field of communications.

II

One of the most revealing statements that can be made about American society in the mid-twentieth century is that in 1959 we shall spend well over $12,000,000,000 on scientific

12

and technical research and development. This is larger than the total national income of many important nations. Even at constant dollars it represents the devotion to research of resources many, many times as great as we devoted to that purpose before World War II.

This fact has deep meaning for many reasons. Until recent years the great advances in pure science were, so far as public policy was concerned, essentially accidental. They were the product of a country gentleman like Darwin driven by curiosity, a lonely monk like Mendel, a patent-office clerk stealing time from his work like Einstein, a doctor whose nagging curiosity would not let him rest after the last patient of the day was treated, a professor not content with teaching. Only a handful of men before World War II were able to devote themselves, free of all other responsibilities, to pure scientific research. Now society devotes tremendous resources to the deliberate and planned prosecution of research. It is no wonder that there has been an explosive growth in the actual *quantity* of knowledge. Fields of knowledge unheard of a generation ago have become complete disciplines in themselves, with journals, societies, chairs and sub-specializations. The reports of research overflow the journals and all the less formal means of publication and present so difficult a problem of organization that one of the most time-consuming elements in any new research project is a search of the literature to discover the state of present knowledge of the subject.

The rate of growth of the quantity of scientific knowledge is almost matched by growth in other fields. The history, literature, arts, economy, and governments of Asian and Middle Eastern countries, for example, have become the objects of a formidable and growing scholarly effort; and the amassing of data in the social and behaviorial sciences has also increased geometrically.

Yet the size of the resources applied to research makes it clear that this leap forward in the quantity of knowledge is not an experience we have just passed through, but rather one on which we are just beginning. It is now as though we were near the mouth of a river that has already widened to an estuary and is about to open into the broad sea itself.

A fundamental characteristic of our present society is, hence, the enormous increase, and the far greater impending increase, in the actual quantity of knowledge it must organize, retain, disseminate and use.

The $12,000,000,000 annual expenditure for research and development reveals something else, and that is our conviction of the immediate practical utility of scientific discovery. Generations, even centuries, might intervene before the work of scientists of an earlier day had a direct effect on the daily activity of the mass of residents of the societies in which they lived. The economy of the time could proceed in comfortable ignorance of their work, which was of interest primarily to those drawn to it by scientific curiosity. Even in our own century, the achievements of a Planck or an Einstein long remained in the domain of pure theory. Not so today. The great majority of our vast research and development expenditure goes not indeed for pure research—an inherently inexpensive operation—but rather to make instant application of its findings in industry, medicine, and defense. The consequence is that new advances in knowledge penetrate swiftly to every sector of life. In varying degrees and adaptations, every new scientific advance must now be communicated to the tens or hundreds of thousands who will in one way or another make use of it in their daily work. Scholarly learning is no longer in a cloister isolated from the world; it enters into every detail of life and must be disseminated in one form or another to a vastly wider audience than even ten or twenty years ago.

Correspondingly, mechanization and automation have been increasingly displacing human employees from occupations de-

14

manding merely routine skills, while creating an enormous demand for literally millions of scientists, technicians, administrators, and other specialists capable of using the new knowledge. Just as effective participation in nineteenth and early twentieth century industrialization required literacy, henceforth effective participation in our economy will increasingly require a high level of scientific and technical learning.

Another consequence of our astounding support of research is that the body of knowledge with which our communications system must cope is not only almost incomparably larger than ever before and must be conveyed to a very much wider audience than ever before, but it is also changing very much more rapidly than ever before. Almost all of the prescriptions that a fifty-year-old doctor writes are for drugs unknown when he was in medical school, and most of the methods of treatment he now uses are novel or greatly changed. The medical knowledge he actually uses in practice, that is, has been communicated to him since he completed his formal education. This is true of most other professions as well.

And it needs to be equally true of citizens. Just as no medical or engineering school of thirty years ago could have equipped its students to practice their professions today, so no university of that time could have equipped a student to be an intelligent citizen today. The issues of politics have changed beyond foreseeing. Who could have thought in 1929 that our destiny a generation later would hang on the control of atomic energy or the partition of Germany, or the silent march of guerillas in the jungles of Laos?

But the change is not only in the issues themselves that confront us. An even more significant change is taking place in the means of analysis by which we seek to understand them. The economics of 1929—or even of 1939—has proved inadequate to understanding the business cycle, or the economy of modern war, or the problems of economic growth in underdeveloped areas. This rapid obsolescence of economic theory is fully matched in political and social theory. The competent citizen has had not only to learn and relearn bewildering bodies of new facts about distant countries, strange governments, and revolutionary scientific innovations; he has had to reconstruct, and more than once, the theoretical framework within which he has organized his thinking about these new situations. Much of our ineffectiveness in dealing with new problems comes from the efforts of middle-aged statesmen to apply to them the economic and political concepts remembered from their college days—concepts now not so much wrong as simply irrelevant.

Obsolesence is a continuing problem, not only with respect to knowledge but with respect to political and social institutions. Society used to have a long time to adjust to technological change; but today science and technology move at such a pace that there is a constant and acute tension between new technological forces and the outmoded institutions within which they must operate. Obvious examples are the absence of any form of government for metropolitan areas or of any governmental means of dealing effectively with water resources or of any sound theory of defense in the nuclear age or of any effective international government. Perhaps even more serious are the many problems so new that we are not yet really aware that we have no solution for them.

In any period of swift change we are frightened by the unfamiliar and are impelled to turn backward from it. There is a resistance to change, and a demand for what a former President called "a return to normalcy." But if anything is certain in so uncertain a world as ours, it is that there can be no return to an untroubled past. Our problems are here, now, instant and demanding. They will be solved, if at all, not by any retreat but **only** by such a burst of social innovation as our society has **never** seen. One of our most urgent needs is to **invite** innovation, to

16

encourage new thought, to seek out and welcome means of change. We massively support scientific and technological research, which have presented us with dilemmas that could lead either to abundance or destruction. We need now to look to the thin advancing edge of political and social and philosophical thought in which lies our hope of resolving those dilemmas.

Just as the advanced technology of our times must be shared by a much larger part of the working force than was the case with scientific knowledge of a generation ago, so the proportion of the population exercising real influence on major issues of national policy and hence needing to share a genuine understanding of those issues has grown. This is measured in part by an increase in voting. But even more important has been the increased facility for arousing and expressing public opinion afforded by the new media of communication. The negotiation of the Treaty of Alliance of 1778 or the Treaty of Paris of 1783 or the Jay Treaty or indeed the drafting of the Constitution itself could proceed without the involvement or even the awareness of more than a small elite of especially well informed leaders. The pressure of public opinion on political action became steadily greater in the latter nineteenth century with the coming of near-universal literacy and the instant and relatively full dissemination of news through the daily press. It was, for example, press-aroused public opinion that drove us into the folly of the Spanish War. Television has added enormously to this pressure. On most important issues, public opinion—no matter how well or ill informed —is now likely to be strong and clamorous, so much so that the freedom of action of those in authority is narrowly limited. During the war a statesman could not have flown in the face of sentiment toward our Russian allies and taken measures which would have limited their post-war power; today it is most difficult, on the contrary, for the statesman to be sufficiently flexible toward Russia to negotiate an easing of tension. The French government until recently has been equally chained by public opinion to an obviously disastrous policy in Algeria; and the American government has very little freedom in its China policy. Senators from states like New York and from states like Arkansas, whatever their personal views, are compelled to positions on school integration and other racial issues that are irrationally hardened.

What I am trying to say is that our governments today cannot be wiser than we are. Public opinion is so easily created and so effectively expressed that it peremptorily defines the boundaries within which a choice of public policies can operate. Wise policies are possible only to the extent that the public understands and will support them. This delimiting role of public opinion has always existed, of course, but never until today has it been a factor of such force. Never until today, in consequence, has the necessity of a continual education of the population at large with respect to major issues been of such critical importance.

And the issues we confront today are increasingly ones which even the most experienced man can know about only at second hand. The issues of independence from imperial control and of slavery and related matters that underlay the Revolution and the Civil War were, heaven knows, complicated enough and difficult enough of decision but at least they lay before mens' eyes in the ambit of their daily experience. But who from his daily experience can estimate the danger of radioactive fall-out from bomb testing, or weigh that danger against the strengthening of our security that might come from further test-aided research? Who from his daily experience can form a judgment of Russian intentions or indeed even know Russia at all? Who, on the basis of his daily experience, can reach sound opinions on the requirements of economic development in South Asia? Yet these are all questions on whose correct answering our lives and indeed our civilization may depend.

The world to which we respond in our political acts is not

18

the real world in all its distant and unknowable complexity, but an envisioned world whose image is formed for us by the daily flow of communication in which we are bathed. On the accuracy and fullness of that popularly held image depend the wisdom and effectiveness of our public policies and the character of the future that flows from them.

Another consequence of the more complex organization of society rising from the wider and more elaborate use of the new technology is that the patterns of everybody's daily behavior are much more completely determined socially. Very many Americans work for very large corporations or governmental agencies with intricate internal organization, and the concept of the "organization man" as one whose whole life is determined by the necessities of adaptation to the corporate organism of which he is a part has become a cliché of our current speech. Yet the social determination of the working activities of the self-employed or the worker for the small company is almost equally great. The individual owner of a small filling station is as definitely "fixed" in the vast pattern of the automotive industry and as dependent on its vagaries as the assembly-line worker at General Motors or the worker in the small independent plant that produces a single GM component on contract. The successful doctor or lawyer, though in private practice, plays a role in a vast network of people and institutions that serve our health or maintain the lawful patterns of our lives, to which he must adapt as much as the executive in an oil company. The truth is that it is our society itself that has become vast and interwoven and we must each fulfill his role in its intricate ecology whether working alone or as a corporate employee with thousands of fellows.

It is pointless to deplore this more highly organized character of contemporary life. It is simply a fact that the enormous sources of power made available to us can be used only by a society with an extremely high degree of specialization of economic functions;

it can only work with, as it were, a highly "orchestrated" performance. Anarchy and disorganization society cannot tolerate; the population has grown too large in relation to the resource base to be sustained except by continuous and well-organized activity. In modern wars the principal cause of death is likely to be not combat but starvation resulting from the disorganization of economic activity.

It is obvious that for each person to perform usefully in so highly organized yet so fluid a society, he must receive a constant flow of information that will enable him to adapt his behavior to the changing requirements. In large part, this information consists of orders or instructions, like those to a locomotive engineer telling him at what hour and minute he is to report at what terminal to take what train where. But even within large corporations, specific instructions have become less and less adequate to bring the activity of employees into the necessary pattern. Certainly they will be far less adequate in the future, as more and more jobs capable of being governed by fixed instructions will be taken over by machines. Increasingly the necessary coordination will be obtained by preparing the employee with sufficient training so that he has a high level of insight into the purposes of his work and will independently make the desired decisions when confronted with unforeseeable circumstances. This method of achieving social adaptation is most complete, of course, in respect to the self-employed professional like the doctor or lawyer. He receives no "orders," yet his long professional training, the careful implantation of professional ethics, and the steady flow through professional journals and meetings of new information means that members of the profession, confronted with a given situation—a contract to be drawn or an appendix to be removed—will respond to it in a more or less uniform or at least similar way and will discharge effectively the social role required of them. More and more it is by similar means that the

20

more responsible employee within a large corporation fits his work to the corporation's needs.

This method of achieving social co-ordination is far more expensive of communication, and of communication of a higher order, than achieving co-ordination by instruction from above. It means that each participant in the common endeavor must understand the whole endeavor and be kept currently informed of the entire changing situation so that he can continuously make his own proper adaptation to it. And he must understand the purposes of the general enterprise and share its values to a degree that will impel him to make that adaptation. These needs will exist whether the enterprise that must be organized is a small business firm or the entire society. Such very large enterprises as our major corporations or the armed services have undertaken elaborate internal programs of training, indoctrination, and current information in order to achieve the higher level of co-ordination now required. In a precisely similar way society itself, to sustain its extremely complex present organization, needs and largely has achieved a massive flow of information whose principal purpose is to enable individuals to fit themselves meaningfully to society's needs and to achieve a sharing of values that will give them a common motivation.

Though in a sense the noncompulsive achievement of co-ordination that is becoming increasingly characteristic of our society liberates the individual from close control, it carries the danger of a subtler and more complete domination. Even though we release a man from the dictation of specific orders and enlarge the area in which he is free to use his best judgment, we do not necessarily increase his liberty if we accompany this action by measures aimed at predetermining his judgment and values. To put it in its simplest terms, a man who was shanghaied into a navy of the the Napoleonic era and enforced to his tasks by a whip in the hands of a boatswain but left to think what he willed may have been a freer man than the one has been led by carefully designed and tested appeals to volunteer and serve with zeal.

I do not mean to suggest that any hidden persuaders at the center of our society are endeavoring in a calculated manner to shape us to their purposes by the use of our communications system in the way that any large corporation openly and no doubt properly tries to shape the working energies of its employees to its purposes. I do mean to say that of necessity, in so highly organized a society as ours, our behavior is shaped into social patterns very largely by a steady flow of communications, and that these tend not only to give us information but to fix the standards of our values. Insofar as the flow of communications emanates from a few sources, unconsciously perhaps sharing common values, the values of those sources will become the common standard toward which we are all drawn. This is not necessarily evil: some community of value and purpose is an indispensable cement of society. The danger lies, I believe, in the degree to which the communication of common values may be pervasive and unexamined in the absence of an effective dissemination of critical or alternative views. Autonomy exists only in the presence of conscious and informed choice.

The communication of values through the newer media assumes, moreover, a special importance in the light of current and prospective changes in our society. The swift scientific advances of this century have a deep philosophical as well as a technological significance. Decades of strain were required before religious thought could accommodate the implications, successively, of the Copernican, Newtonian, and Darwinian revolutions, an accommodation achieved in each case at the expense of a considerable area of earlier orthodoxy. The implications of twentieth-century science promise to be even more sweeping. We may mention but four of these. Though the geocentric conception of the physical arrangement of the universe was discredited by the Copernican the-

22

ory and the telescopic revelation of the vast number of stars, the philosophical impact was relatively small so long as the earth was believed to retain the center of the Divine attention as the unique site of life. Recent discoveries which suggest that the biological experiment is probably under way on vast, even infinite, numbers of planets will probably provide the most shattering of the new scientific insights when their implications are generally perceived. In the second place, a conception of a palpable "substance" modified in various ways as the ultimate material reality has had to yield to a concept of reality as merely a configuration of energy. The Newtonian concept of unvarying cause and effect, which had to a degree replaced the intervention of Divine providence as an order-creating principle in our conceptions of the universe, has lost its philosophical rigidity in the fact of Heisenberg's demonstration of inherent uncertainties and the statistical and probabilistic conception of natural law. And finally Freudian insights have greatly altered the conception of the nature of man himself. Though only the last of these has yet penetrated popular thought to any degree, one can hardly overestimate the ultimate consequence of scientific perceptions that in one half-century have dissolved our conception of reality, melted the rigid framework of space and time into an interchangeable flux, reduced certitude to a statistical probability, robbed us of our unique role in creation, and burst through the flattering surface images of our own character.

Simultaneously the greater mobility of society has lessened the role of the traditional institutions through which fundamental and unconsciously assumed values have been implanted—the family, the community, the rooted inheritance of outlook. This is not necessarily in itself undesirable. Our ability to maintain a meaningful value system is likely to depend more on our ability to adapt to the newer concepts of the universe and of reality than on our success in preserving traditional outlooks, and a strengthening of change-oriented value sources at the expense of tradition-oriented sources is probably desirable. But it does mean that among the responsibilities of the communications system we require is a much greater role in value formation than the media have previously had, and at a time when values are in an extraordinary state of flux.

III

Perhaps we are now in a position to define some of the characteristics that the changing nature of our society requires in the communications system:

1. That system must be able to record and organize for recall a very much greater body of knowledge than our society has ever before used or indeed now possesses. It must do so though the difficulty of recording and organizing a growing body of facts increases not arithmetically but geometrically. Each new element of knowledge must be handled not only in itself but in its relations with all other elements of knowledge, so that to deal with one hundred thousand pieces of information is far more than one hundred times as big a job as to deal with one thousand pieces.

2. It must be able to convey to a mass audience information of a high order of complexity such as has before been shared by a rather small elite. Universal literacy and the universal distribution of simple printed matter were indispensable bases of late nineteenth-century industrial democracy. In the same way, an indispensable basis for the society developing in this century is a comparably wide dissemination of organized knowledge at the college or university level.

3. It must make possible the continuing education or re-education of adults to a degree never before necessary.

4. To permit the co-ordination of our increasingly complex society, it must multiply the flow of current information or

24

"news," in quantity, in depth and complexity, and in the number of people to be kept informed.

5. As a protection against the acute danger of an oversimplification or misrepresentation of problems now perceived almost wholly at second-hand through the media of communication, the communications system must provide the maximum possible opportunity for the dissemination of minority, divergent, and critical comment, and must amplify the individual's opportunity to receive a diversity of information and points of view that can challenge and test the accuracy and fullness of the dominant image of those problems.

6. The crisis resulting from the increasingly serious lag between the rate of governmental and institutional change on the one hand, and the rate of scientific and technological change on the other, makes it essential that the communications system do everything possible to encourage, nourish, and disseminate new ideas and novel approaches to their solution.

7. In the philosophical disorder of our times, and in view of the unusual dependence on the media for the derivation of values and philosophic insights, it is important that our communications system be able to afford something more than the shallow and vacuous re-echoing of the forms of traditional beliefs, and provide substance for the individual hammering out of new insights. It must nourish the autonomous development of individual value rather than the anxious facility to conform.

Chapter **II** *The Response*

Our society has moved vigorously to meet the urgent demands upon the American communication system. Its responses have taken the form of technical devices, institutional organization, and commitment of resources.

Of first importance has been the educational response. Fundamental to any communications system is the kind of education to which it is related. It is in the school itself that much of the actual communication of organized knowledge takes place; and more importantly, it is the school that equips to communicate. The teaching of writing was as essential a part of the leap to civilization as its invention; the extension of literacy to the generality of the upper classes was of concomitant importance with the beginning of printing; and universal education and power printing were linked developments of the nineteenth century.

The characteristic educational development of our generation is the extension of college training to a large portion of the entire population. Though much of the tremendous increase in college enrollments foreseen for the next twenty years will come simply from an increase in the college-age population, almost all of the increase that has occurred to date has represented a rise in the proportion of young men and women who receive college training. Between 1890 and 1950, the percentage of the population

26

graduating annually from college increased ten-fold, and it is continuing to rise rapidly. A continuation of present trends will produce by another generation or two a population about half of which will be college trained—a figure approaching, perhaps exceeding, the maximum number capable of college-level work.

Of equal or greater significance is the even more rapid increase in the proportion of the population receiving post-graduate training. More than twice as many advanced degrees were conferred in 1950 as in 1940, and the figure is continuing to increase. And within any given level of college or university training, for all our concern with present shortcomings, the sheer quantity of information conveyed is likely to be much greater than a generation ago. A doctor or engineer or Ph.D. in economics or an ordinary A.B. in political science emerging from the university today simply is likely to know more than his fellow of a quarter of a century ago.

Meanwhile, high school training, which a generation ago reached about the proportion of the population that college does today, has moved to the level of universality that the elementary school has occupied since the latter nineteenth century.

Our educational system has responded reasonably well not only to the need for a far wider sharing of advanced knowledge, but also to the necessity of handling a much larger and more complex body of information. University curricula have, for example, greatly expanded their offering in Russian and Asian studies and new courses in physics, biochemistry, and related fields follow hard on the opening of new areas to research. Indeed the advance of knowledge is now largely in the hands of the academic community, which in the preceding century was remote from most pioneering research.

It has not responded well, however, to the need for graduating students prepared for the continuous self-education or re-education made necessary by the rapid obsolescence of knowledge.

27

Such studies as *Reading for Life* [1] demonstrate depressingly the non-reading of university graduates.

Indeed, to teach what-is-known remains the unquestioned objective of most education, which sometimes seems hardly aware of a responsibility to train students to learn what-will-come-to-be-known. College students now graduating will spend far more of their waking hours reading books, newspapers, and magazines, listening to radio, and watching television and movies than in any activity save maintaining a home or making a living. Their working hours as well will increasingly be devoted to using one or another of these means of communications. How effectively they read and listen and watch will determine the usefulness of their work, the rightness of their political decisions, and even the maintenance of their own integrity. Yet very little of our educational effort is devoted to training them to carry on this continuing self-education or even to convincing them that it is important.

II

Within the communications system more narrowly defined, our times have seen two major sets of technical developments, each of truly revolutionary potential and each extending the spectrum of communications possibilities beyond the range of print.

One set is designed to solve the problems of storing and organizing the vast quantities of data now embodied in recorded knowledge and the far vaster quantities that must be handled in the daily control of technological and administrative processes. This set of developments includes a number of devices for reproducing texts in miniature to simplify their handling and reduce the cost

[1] Jacob M. Price, editor, *Reading for Life*, Ann Arbor, University of Michigan Press, 1959.

28

of their storage. Of these, the most familiar is microfilm, but there are many more recent devices making possible the printing in miniature of substantial numbers of copies. Another kind of device is that permitting data to be automatically recorded, sorted, selected, or employed in computation. Such are the now relatively primitive punch-card machines capable of performing these processes on data recorded by patterns of holes in cards that activate electric circuits. Much more sophisticated are the computers that act on data reduced to binary digits and recorded as electromagnetic pulses on wire or tape.

These devices are of great importance, especially when bulky and rarely used materials must be preserved in several, but not a great many, copies, and when a very large quantity of data must be rearranged several times or selected in varying permutations, but when each arrangement or selection is to be used only once or rarely. Without them the clerical work required by contemporary business, military, and governmental organization simply could not be carried on. Some have foreseen the possibility that such devices, used in combination, could totally revolutionize the library.

Perhaps typical of the more extravagant comments is the following from a special article by Maurice B. Mitchell on "A Forward Look at Communications" in the 1958 *Britannica Yearbook:*

The problems of providing space for books in libraries and the deterioration of books through use and age will be overcome by the resources of the microfilm camera and the electronic brain. While the microfilm camera copies or records millions of pages of printed texts, the electronic brain will analyze them and index and cross-index them under appropriate headings.

Tomorrow's researcher, in the comfort of his office, will be able to scan through the pertinent writings in any subject area in a fraction of the time it would otherwise take by simply asking the library's electronic brain to bring forth the answers to any questions. High-speed electronic printers at every microfilm reader will make reproductions of this data immediately available.[2]

Unhappily, our problems are not so easily solved. It is still ordinarily much cheaper to build storage space for any given body of documents than to microfilm them, and any mode of reproduction that makes a document illegible without large special reading machines is obviously impractical for purposes of general communication. And even the magic capacities for arrangement and selection possessed by the mightiest electronic brains solve only the easiest part of the problem. Our visions of a machine that will produce all the world's literature on any given subject at the push of a button will work only if human eyes and brains and hands have first coded under the appropriate subject heading all the relevant references in the world's literature. If one had the resources to do all the fantastically detailed subject cataloging tacitly assumed in all the descriptions of electronic marvels, a conventional subject catalog would work about as well.

The other great set of new developments is in the field of wireless broadcasting. Radio became a practical means of broadcasting public communication shortly after World War I; television shortly after World War II. By mid-century our immersion in the broadcast media was complete.

There were 87,800,000 radio sets and 49,300,000 television receivers in the United States by 1958; 97 per cent of all homes had radios, most of them two or more, and 83 per cent had television sets, with the latter figure rising rapidly. These household sets were augmented by 58 million portable and automobile radios, so that almost no American needed ever to be beyond the flow of broadcast words and images. About 3,200 radio stations

[2] *Encyclopaedia Britannica,* editors, *1958 Britannica Book of the Year,* William Benton, publisher, 1958, p. 55.

30

and 500 television stations provided a continuous service, reaching with radio into every corner, and with television into almost every corner, of the United States.

By 1957 it was estimated that the average adult American was spending about 30 hours a week listening or viewing, a total of more than 1,500 hours per person per year. No single activity except work and sleep—not even eating—consumed so large a proportion of the time of Americans. There were also marked changes in the more traditional media of communication, influenced in part by these electronic developments.

III

The motion picture, a creature of the earlier years of the century, had also grown rapidly and became for a time the principal entertainment of Americans, as measured in hours spent. Though surpassed in the inter-war years by radio, it continued to grow in weekly attendance until the beginning of national television broadcasting in the late 1940's. Though this brought a sharp decline in weekly motion-picture theater attendance from about 80,000,000 in 1948 to little more than 42,000,000 in 1958, it actually vastly increased the audience for films, which came to make up a high proportion of television programming. In addition to the 80,000,000 man-hours a week still spent in the motion picture theater, an indeterminate portion of the several billion man-hours a week spent before the TV screen was devoted to watching the product of Hollywood, which had never before reached so many Americans so intimately or so pervasively.

Among the traditional media of communication, newspapers lagged. Circulation increased, but hardly more than the population, so that by 1958 the newspaper circulation per family was no larger than in 1940. Each issue of the newspaper was likely to be larger than a generation ago; but the increase was almost entirely in advertising, which occupied 60 per cent of the average newspaper in 1958, as contrasted with 40 per cent 18 years earlier. The dissemination of news and other editorial content per capita is certainly relatively, and probably absolutely, less than in prewar years.

Contraction in the newspaper field was also observed in the declining number of independent papers. The number of daily newspapers in the United States declined steadily from the turn of the century onward, from 2,190 in 1900 to 1,760 in 1955. Combination of ownership also became steadily more common so that by 1955, 93 chains controlled 427, or about one-fourth, of the daily newspapers. It also became common for one owner to control a morning and an evening newspaper—frequently, even usually, the only two in the same city. As a result of this contraction, of the 1,452 cities in the U.S. with daily newspapers, only 89 have more than one independently owned paper.

Magazines had a much more vigorous growth both in number and in circulation. As in the case of newspapers, but to a perhaps even more marked degree, there was an increase in the proportion of the space in magazines devoted to advertising and in the financial dependence on advertising revenue. This was a consequence of the growth of trademarked or otherwise nationally indentified products seeking a national market.

Two other aspects of the growth of magazines were notable. One was the vigorous response to the need for conveying a much larger flow of scientific, technical, and scholarly knowledge. Hundreds of new journals were founded in these fields.

The other new development of really major importance was the rise of news magazines. By the late nineteenth century the invention of the power rotary press, rail carriage of the mails, and low geographically uniform postal rates had made possible the national magazine as we know it; but not until the 1920's were manufacture (especially of illustrated material) and distri-

32

bution so speeded up as to enable the magazine to serve as a carrier of current news. The solution of many of these technical problems enabled first *Time,* then *Newsweek, United States News and World Report,* and *Life* and many more specialized magazines, such as *The Reporter* or *Business Week,* to enter this field. By 1959 the four principal general weekly news magazines alone (including *Life*) enjoyed a combined weekly circulation of more than 10,000,000.

Books, too, responded to the demand for increased communication. The new titles published annually in the United States rose from 5,400 in 1900 to 11,000 in 1958. A whole new body of publishers—the university presses—had come into existence. The handful of university "presses" functioning in 1900, none of which were real publishing enterprises in a proper sense, had grown by 1959 over 50, which published annually about 1,400 books and made them available not merely to the scholarly community but to the whole national book market.

The traditional methods of book distribution were supplemented in the mid-twentieth century by two new devices, the book club and the mass-distributed paperbound book. Both of these were adaptations of distribution methods worked out for magazines: advance subscription with mail delivery in the case of the book club, and wholesaler distribution to newsstand outlets in the case of the paperbound books. By 1958 well over half of all adult books, other than textbooks and encyclopedias, were sold through these two channels.

IV

There could be no complaint of the quantitive enlargement of the American communications system in response to the twentieth-century demand. At the present time the average American probably spends about 35 hours a week listening to radio, watching television or films, or reading books, newspapers, and magazines. This is well over half of all the time free after work, sleep, and eating. The production of the material consumed in this voracious reception of communications occupies one of our greatest assemblages of industries, with an employment of well over 1,000,000 persons and a total annual budget of several billion dollars.

The average American remains "plugged in" to his culture for a major part of all his free hours, receiving an endless flow of entertainment and information. The opportunity is certainly present for him to receive all of the information he could conceivably need to meet the new demands of his time. Indeed, so massive and continuous is his exposure to communication that a new set of problems is created, relating not to the "under-reception" of information, but rather to "over-reception" to such a degree that vicarious experience dominates direct experience and the uncritical acceptance of a projected image may drown out the development of autonomous judgment and cultural individuality. Certainly the very massiveness of the organized flow of communications makes the character of its content and the independence of the citizen-receiver's relation to it decisive both of our national strength and of our individual freedoms.

How well this enormously enlarged engine of communication serves the needs described earlier depends in part on certain technological and economic characteristics of the various media of communication and in part on the way in which they are organized and administered. Some of the relevant questions are: How large an audience, assembled under what circumstances, is required to make a communication economically feasible? Who pays for a communication and how? How much investment is required to establish a communications service—that is, to establish a publishing house or a magazine or a broadcasting station? In particular, is it necessary to own the physical facilities—the

34

presses or film studios or transmitters—to "publish" through them? How many different communications is it technically or economically feasible to offer in one community at once?

Let us examine some of these questions briefly with respect to the individual media, and then return to a consideration of how well the system as a whole meets its responsibilities.

V

One of the most important of all factors affecting the role of any medium of communications is the ratio between the initial cost of producing a message—that is, a broadcast, a film, or a book or magazine or newspaper issue—and the added cost of making each additional copy or adding each listener or viewer. At one extreme, of course, is the handwritten document, very cheap to produce in a single copy but costing almost as much for each additional copy as for the first. Its communications use is hence largely confined to personal letters, intended for a single reader.

At the opposite extreme is that most dramatic of the newer media: television. A television station is very expensive to build, and yet more expensive to operate. Its broadcast signal can be received only within a limited radius, so that any program offered to a national audience must be broadcast over a network of dozens of stations with costly cable connections. The production of a program with lighting and sets and rehearsals costs much more than on radio. The costs of a full hour evening network show, including time of all the participating stations, will run at least $200,000, and may be very much more; and even a modest network performance at daytime rates will cost $65,000 or more an hour.

Costs of this order make television inefficient and almost prohibitively expensive for very small audiences. This is true regardless of whether television is privately or publicly managed, or in what way it is financed.

On the other hand, once a program is on the air the cost is unchanging, whether one person views it or ten million. This fact makes television, like radio, an extremely efficient way of reaching the vast audiences its most popular programs are able to draw. It is by no means uncommon for a program to attract an audience of several tens of millions, which means that even the most expensive show costs well under a nickel a person an hour, far less than the cost of books, newspapers, magazines, or films. It is natural therefore for television, under any management, to seek the largest mass audience, for which it is technologically best adapted.

This tendency has been greatly accentuated in this country by the way in which television is organized and financed. When public radio broadcasting was begun in the United States, it was at the cost of manufacturers of radio receivers, who sought, by offering popular broadcasts, to create a market for their sets. The broadcasts created a market for their competitor's sets as well, and other means of financing had to be sought. The aversion to governmental participation in communications or indeed in any business activity, especially strong in the 1920's, and the familiar precedent of advertising support of newspapers and magazines perhaps made it inevitable that the expanding broadcasting system should support itself by selling time for advertising. This precedent carried naturally over into television.

Advertising support has had a special impact on broadcasting for several reasons. A national television program aimed at any special market—purchasers of surgical instruments, for example, or tennis rackets, or hunting rifles—would cost just as much to produce and broadcast as a general program viewed by hundreds of times as many people. Networks for this reason have to charge any specialized advertiser a sum that would be for him prohibi-

36

tive. Network advertising is hence feasible only for products like beer, cigarettes, cosmetics, and automobiles that have a universal market. Such advertisers in turn demand the largest possible audience on a relatively indiscriminate basis, and thereby reinforce the natural propensity of TV to do mass-appeal programming.

In the second place, broadcasting—in contrast to newspapers and magazines—is totally supported by advertising. No program can securely exist, whatever its other excellencies, unless it meets the somewhat specialized test of being able to assemble an audience receptive to the advertising appeals of a particular product and so very large, even in relation to the necessarily high cost of broadcasting, that the cost per listener is very low.

Finally, the advertiser in a newspaper or magazine has no responsibility for the content of anything but his own advertisement, and he generally has no control over the placement of his message within the publication unless he has paid an extra price for one of the regularly offered premium positions. This is not the case in broadcasting, in which the sponsor generally assumes entire responsibility for the program on which his product is advertised. Not only is he in a position to demand a program that will attract an enormous audience, he can also insist that its content will not arouse resentments or antagonisms that might attach to him or his product, but will rather induce in the audience a mood that will make them receptive to the advertising appeal. The situation is much as if every article or story in a magazine were written by or to the order of the purchaser of adjacent advertising space with the sole objective of providing the best "frame" for his advertising message.

The exceptions to advertising domination are, of course, unsponsored "sustaining" programs broadcast by networks or local stations as a public service and news broadcasts and panel discussions by political and other leaders, which, though usually sponsored, remain free of the advertisers' control. The sustaining programs are often of high quality, or present important news coverage—as of political conventions or Presidential addresses. Usually, however, such programs—unless they record important events that fix their own time—are relegated to hours of limited viewing for which there are few buyers available. Sunday afternoon in particular has come to be known as the intellectual ghetto of broadcasting.

With these exceptions, the content of the whole vast flow that daily absorbs so many scores of millions of hours of the attention of Americans is almost wholly determined by advertisers' needs. These needs are by themselves by no means evil or vicious. If the sponsor has little motive to inform or uplift his audience, neither has he any purpose to indoctrinate or control them. The only objective of his own he seeks to impose on the audience is the simple and overt one expressed in the commercial. Otherwise, he anxiously seeks out the audiences' wishes, painfully counting noses and measuring responses to assure himself that the program he offers appeals to the maximum possible number of millions, fits comfortably into their preconceptions, and leaves them in a relaxed and responsive mood.

The pressure for sheer size of audience is almost unbelievably great. Though a book or a specialized magazine could be made available nationally if there were 5,000 or even fewer buyers assembled over a period of time—in the case of a book over a year or more—a television program can be made nationally available on a prime viewing time only if an audience of many millions can reasonably certainly be assembled *at one time* to view the offering. Since the size of the audience does not affect the cost of the broadcast, even a potential audience of 5,000,000 can not be assured of having their interests served at a given hour if some different kind of program could draw a couple of million more.

The frustration of minority interests—even those of minority

38

audiences large beyond the dreams of book and most magazine publishers—is greatly increased by limitations on the numbers of stations. For technical reasons, so long as television remains confined to the frequency range in which commercial telecasts take place, only 6 or 7 channels can be used simultaneously in a given area. Nor can one, as in AM or short-wave radio, tune to a distant station. In most areas of the United States the choice of a television viewer is in practice confined to two or three alternatives, and in many communities only one station can be received.

The consequence of these technological and organizational factors is that the overwhelming content of network television during prime listening hours consists of light entertainment, intellectually undemanding and carefully disengaged from controversial issues. In a week in October, 1959, chosen at random, the evening offering from 7:00 to 11:00 P.M. of the three major networks included:

$18\frac{1}{2}$ hours of crime and detective plays
16   hours of very light drama series
$15\frac{1}{2}$ hours of variety
$14\frac{1}{2}$ hours of westerns
$2\frac{1}{2}$ hours of sport programs
$2\frac{1}{2}$ hours of quiz programs
$2\frac{1}{2}$ hours of more serious drama
$2\frac{1}{2}$ hours of news
2   hours of humor
1   hour of movies
1   hour of science fiction
1   hour of "science" by Walt Disney
1   hour of music

Science news has been estimated at less than $\frac{1}{4}$ per cent of broadcast time.

Programs of this sort undoubtedly respond to the majority demand, and it is noteworthy that quite similar programs make up an important part of the telecasts of the noncommercial BBC. The point is rather that the technology and economics of television tend to reinforce the majority taste so that it acquires an almost exclusive dominance. If of the audience for Wednesday evening drama 70 per cent prefer westerns, 20 per cent serious contemporary drama, and 10 per cent classic drama, the network will be under great pressure to be 100 per cent western. Though the situation is somewhat better in off-hours, there is at peak viewing hours a serious underrepresentation of the cultural interests of any but a lowest-common-denominator majority. Nor are these neglected minorities small, eccentric, or esoteric. Even though there may be a million persons eager to see a given kind of play, and even though they may be quite willing to pay for the privilege a sum in the aggregate far more than the cost of producing and broadcasting such a show, there is now almost no way in which a group no larger than that could have its wish satisfied on an evening network broadcast. Among the almost inevitable consequences of the present technology and economic organization of television is an overwhelming preoccupation with entertainment and a high degree of uniformity, banality, and superficiality in the entertainment offered. Other consequences that may have an even greater significance relate to television's dealings with social, economic, and political issues. These are manifest, of course, both implicitly in entertainment programs and explicitly in news and discussion programs. The former occupy a far greater portion of the broadcast hours and are potentially the more important in their effect on audience attitudes. It should be evident from the preceding discussion that no significant social criticism is likely in broadcast drama. Personal emotional problems may be explored with some perceptiveness and integrity, but rarely will a televised play call in question the currently popular assumptions of society, be a force for change, or offend accepted views.

40

In public events programs there is controversy enough. Every major point of view can find expression on every issue already recognized to be an issue, and about which the public is already concerned. The panel discussion, even the unsponsored sustaining program, is itself under great pressure to capture an audience of millions, and this is thought possible only if already well-known "personalities" are debating issues already chewed over to the point of familiarity. Though the debaters on the panel may pummel each other with a lusty and heated verbosity, their dialogue takes place only within a narrow framework of already accepted terms and values. Most of the familiar political questions that will be talked about from the screen during the untold hundreds of millions of manhours of listening during any presidential campaign will be already obsolete and the answers reiterated not right or wrong but simply meaningless. The emerging problems that our future hangs upon, and the first openings toward their solution, will not be on the television screen because there will be no way in which millions can yet have become enough aware of them to be interested.

In the face of all of these difficulties imposed by the technology of television itself and by the pattern of organization and support into which it stumbled, it is a tribute to the not easily suppressed creativity of those who work in the medium that there are frequent broadcasts with freshness and charm and excitement. Growing technical and artistic resources are apparent, and there are programs now and again that suggest almost breathtakingly what television might be. It is also perhaps a comment on the barrenness of the cultural life most Americans have led that even the banal fare of day-to-day viewing has opened for them new and wider worlds of interest. And yet this is undoubtedly true.

Especially valuable have been the televising of actual events—political conventions, campaign speeches, Congressional hearings, Presidential addresses, a Khrushchev visit. No other force, I believe, can account for the remarkable stimulus of interest in politics shown, for example, in the increase in voting in the last few years. Voting in Presidential elections had been relatively stable at 46 to 49 million from 1936 through 1948; but in 1952, after the first extensively televised campaign, it jumped by nearly 30 per cent and has remained at the higher level, though the later campaigns were neither closely nor very bitterly contested. Certainly no other medium can present public figures themselves so directly and revealingly to the mass of citizens.

The very fact that television is usually so passively received means it will often bring to the viewer programs about subjects of which he was previously unaware or in which he was uninterested, as contrasted with the case of the reader who must actively seek out a book in a library or bookstore and will not often do so unless his interest has already been drawn to the work or its subject. Television has an enormous potential in initially capturing attention and introducing the viewer to areas new to him.

VI

Much of what has been said of television is true of radio. Even more of it was true twelve to fifteen years ago when radio dominated broadcasting. The important current trends in radio have come principally as an adjustment to television. And one or two of them may foreshadow future developments in the latter medium. The economic organization of radio is very close to that of television. Indeed the same networks dominate both, and local radio and television stations more often than not have a common owner. Both are almost entirely supported by advertising revenue.

The principal technological and economic differences are:

1. It is much cheaper to build a small local radio station than

42

a TV station and very much cheaper to operate and produce programs for it.

2. The availability of a whole new band of FM frequencies has made possible both the opening of a number of new, inexpensive stations of local broadcasting range and a great improvement in the quality and fidelity with which music is transmitted.

3. The preference of national advertisers for television as the medium for their heavy investments has lessened the importance of network radio. A much higher proportion of radio shows are now locally sponsored and originated.

4. The availability of excellent and inexpensive transcriptions has enabled the small local station to maintain programs of adequate or even very high quality at small expense.

5. The preemption by television of most of the audience who devote an evening to broadcast listening has tended to leave radio the audience who want music as a background for something else—housework, studying, dancing—or whose activities—driving, picnicking, sunbathing—take them beyond the range of television. It has also left radio the small but important audience of those seriously interested in music and in discussions not able to draw a large enough audience for television.

The consequence of these forces has been a high degree of decentralization, with local stations responding rather inexpensively and unusually unimaginatively to undemanding local desires. Expensive entertainment programs done with a high degree of professional polish for network performance have largely migrated to television. Though radio continues to broadcast major political addresses, hearings, and conventions and similar public events, it is largely as a by-product of their televising, and the screen is the public's favored way of receiving them.

The removal of some of the pressure for enormous national audiences, and of the sources of financial support for programs designed to attract such audiences, has allowed radio in some respects to drift downward to a lower and less expensive level of banality, with a continuous playing of rock-and-roll records interspersed with strident used-car commercials being only too characteristic of the programs of many local stations. The removal of the same pressures, however, coupled with economic and technological developments favoring small local stations, has given radio an opportunity to show what it can do with serious music. In the larger metropolitan areas the best of the whole world of music is almost continually available, and this has had important consequences for the whole level of musical taste and interest in the United States. And on some stations in some cities there has also been a significant increase in the opportunities for the treatment of unhackneyed issues and ideas, and for critical and leisurely discussions. One has the feeling that if the excitement of television had not drained the older medium of some of its more imaginative creative talent this might indeed be a golden period for radio, and that some of our best communications opportunities are being missed in that medium.

VII

The motion picture industry of the 1930's was almost wholly devoted to entertainment of a very superficial sort. A handful of major studios were responsible for most film production, and each of them was compelled to produce a steady flow of feature films of whatever quality to keep its expensive production facilities employed. A great many motion picture theaters, especially the larger city theaters, were owned by the producing companies; and the economic structure of the industry was such that even the independently owned theaters, under "block-booking" arrangements, were more or less compelled to accept the run of studio output.

This economic structure was itself tolerant of **mediocrity**.

44

Moreover, it enabled the major studios, acting in concert, to enforce both among themselves and against outside companies and importers of foreign films strict compliance with a moral code. This code went far beyond the banning of obscenity and prescribed the treatment (or non-treatment) of many fundamental social problems: marriage, divorce, adultery, prostitution, homosexuality, abortion, illegitimacy, and sexual problems generally; narcotics addiction, use of alcohol, police methods, and attitudes toward police, religion, the clergy, race, and so on and on. Compliance with the code necessarily falsified the films' dealing with many, perhaps most, of the fundamental issues that move men.

The "movies" provided an obviously welcome respite of entertainment to the 80,000,000 or more persons who weekly paid to attend the theater, but one had a feeling of a vast waste of enormous resources of talent and of technical achievement.

The postwar years brought many changes. A series of antitrust cases, initiated earlier, restricted block-booking and ended producer ownership of chains of theaters. Undoubtedly even more important, the rise of television drained away much of the movie theater audience, and particularly that part that merely wanted to while away an evening "seeing a movie." Weekly theater attendance fell by more than half and would have fallen lower but for the rise of drive-in theaters.

These economic changes had important consequences for the content of films. Production was no longer dominated by studios producing routine films to keep their facilities occupied and placing them in controlled outlets. Only distinctive films were likely to attract audiences into the theater, and perhaps the majority of these were produced by independent companies that rented studio facilities and contracted for distribution services. Committed to no overhead, they were able to make as few pictures as they liked and to concentrate on quality. Usually they expressed the creative ability of a single producer or a small team.

Quite small independents with relatively little capital were enabled to enter production, bringing their own ideas. The divorce of a great deal of production from the ownership of manufacturing and distributing facilities paralleled the situation in book and magazine publishing with the same healthy consequences.

The decentralization of production and theater ownership removed the sanctions that had made possible rigid enforcement of the Hollywood code. The code was relaxed in many ways and was not applied at all to many imported films. The result was an adult and honest treatment of social issues that previously could have been dealt with only hypocritically if at all. In such productions as *On the Waterfront, Room at the Top,* or *The Bicycle Thief,* the film gained some of the stature of the legitimate theater as a means of social criticism.

Though much of the production facilties of the Hollywood industry remained devoted to grinding out film for television and horror films and similar trivia—largely apparently for teenagers who wanted to get away from the family circle around the TV screen—one could feel that by the late 1950's the commercial film in the United States, for all its reduced theater audience, had attained a new artistic and social significance.

Meanwhile educational films came into much wider use in consequence of their success as a teaching medium in the enormous job of training members of the World War II armed services. Their postwar use in schools, libraries, and adult educational activities was greatly increased. This use was reinforced by the National Defense Education Act of 1958, which made federal funds available for films along with other non-textbook materials used in teaching science, mathematics, and modern foreign languages in public elementary and secondary schools. An even more important provision of that act for the long run may well be another section that makes funds available for research in

46

the educational uses of radio, television, films, and other audio-visual materials, and for disseminating information about their use.

VIII

Changes in the economic organization of the magazine industry were even more significant in their influence than the technological developments that made possible the news magazines. As in the case of broadcasting, most magazine publishing became dominated economically by its service as an advertising medium. This development had begun in the late nineteenth century, but by the mid-twentieth century it had come to have an almost overwhelming importance. As it was put by Theodore Peterson, "In essence, magazine publishing came to consist of the publisher's deciding on a consumer group which advertisers wished to reach, devising an editorial formula to attract and hold it, and then selling advertisers access to it." [3]

In the case of the mass consumer magazines, competing to reach a relatively undifferentiated mass national audience, some of the consequences resembled those in broadcasting. Particularly was it true that within any competitive field the magazine with the largest readership and a reputation as the most effective advertising medium had an enormous advantage over its less fortunate competitors, even though they might have what under ordinary circumstances would be considered a very large readership indeed. Advertising revenues gravitated to the biggest medium thus depriving its rivals of the financial resources that would enable them to compete for the best editorial content and hence for circulation. This situation was likely to produce a downward spiral that ultimately spelled failure for the less successful competitor, and an upward spiral that produced ever greater dominance for the

[3] Theodore Peterson, *Magazines in the Twentieth Century*, University of Illinois Press, 1956, p. 64.

successful one. Many general-interest magazines failed in this way because their circulation, though absolutely quite large, was not such as to enable them to compete successfully for advertising—*Liberty, American,* and *Collier's* among them. Similarly in the news magazine field the *Literary Digest* passed away entirely and news magazines whose editorial formula did not attract a mass readership, like the *Reporter,* the *Nation,* or the *New Republic,* had financial difficulties in spite of their much lower editorial, production, and circulation costs.

Nevertheless, there were important differences. In the first place, the advertiser had no control over the editorial content of the issue, in contrast with his complete control over the content of programs, other than news programs, sponsored over radio or television. Though the editorial content of mass circulation magazines was carefully shaped to try to attract and hold the particular audience that each magazine's advertisers wanted to reach and thus produced in some cases a somewhat contrived and formula-dominated product, the absence of a public sense of advertiser responsibility for editorial content permitted a greater freedom. Articles could risk irritating some readers without the irritation rubbing off on the adjacently advertised product. Articles could take sides on controversial issues without its being thought that they were expressing views of a sponsor. A preoccupation with effect on a potential customer's attitude did not so firmly overlie creative effort.

In the second place, the fact that so large a part of the cost of a magazine issue was directly dependent on the number of copies distributed (in contrast to broadcasting, where the cost was not affected by the number of listeners) made it economically quite feasible to address a magazine to a small audience with special interests. The advertiser of a product with a limited and specialized market could hence reach his potential buyers throughout the country with inexpensive advertising that did not have to bear

48

the cost of broadcasting to millions of persons whom he did not need to reach. Indeed, the nationally circulated but specialized magazine afforded the only advertising medium, other than direct mail, for reaching a limited but nationwide market; and such journals could command a disproportionately high price per copy for advertising space. As a result, it was easy to provide appropriate magazines for any specialized group of readers that made up a homogeneous market. This was especially significant for the various professional groups of physicians, engineers, executives, and technical experts of all sorts. Thanks to specialized advertising, such professions were abundantly provided with journals which became their principal means for continuing education and for remaining abreast of the rapid developments in their fields.

This economic pattern worked well for the groups who made up a specialized market on the basis of their specialized interests. It served less well those who were interested in poetry, or history, or short stories, and who did not, by virtue of those interests, make up a meaningful market for any particular class of products. But even for such readers, magazines were made possible by the fact that purchasers and subscribers bore a part of this cost. Any interested group that was willing through a higher subscription or newsstand price to pay a higher share could make up for whatever deficiencies existed in advertising revenue. For years readers paid the entire cost of so general a magazine as the *Reader's Digest,* and specialized magazines like *Foreign Affairs,* learned journals, and the various "small" literary reviews receive only limited advertising revenue, while *American Heritage* and *Horizon* receive none. Even such magazines of relatively large circulation as *Harper's* and the *Atlantic Monthly,* whose advertising revenues are probably not sufficient for their high editorial costs, are able to sustain their superior service to their readers by charging two or three times as much per copy as the mass circulated weeklies.

In the third place, no technical limitations on the number of publications existed, as in the number of channels available for broadcasting. Anyone was free to start a magazine who could afford the gamble. And though the cost of starting a mass circulated magazine primarily dependent on advertising revenue would be formidable indeed, the economic organization of the industry was such as to hold costs relatively low, particularly for magazines with limited objectives. Harland Logan in 1949 estimated the cost for a new publisher to start a new magazine aimed at a large national circulation and dependent primarily on advertising revenue at from \$2,000,000 to \$15,000,000, depending on the type of magazine, and calculated the odds as being in most cases rather heavily against success, even with capital in those amounts. Certainly the comparable figures would be substantially higher today.

But one content with small beginnings could start with much less. One of the more significant characteristics of the magazine industry and the book industry, as distinguished from broadcasting and newspapers, is that the function of publishing—the decision as to what is to be emitted and the assumption of the corresponding financial risk—is dissociated from the ownership of the physical means of production—in this case from the printing plant. With a few major exceptions, most magazines hire their printing done. This greatly reduces the amount of capital required to enter the industry and frees the publisher of the necessity of maintaining a certain level of circulation in order to keep his presses occupied. Nor is it necessary to set up a large and expensive distribution machinery in order to make the magazine nationally available. Any one of a dozen or more national distributors will probably be willing to set up its circulation through 850 local wholesalers, and circulation agencies are prepared to undertake to build up subscriptions. The overwhelming majority of magazines have fewer than ten employees. Also, the fact that

50

national distributors pay promptly for their copies received and that subscribers' payments are available in advance lessens the amount of working capital that must be laid out. Many dozens of new magazines are enabled to enter business annually because of this economic structure. Most of them fail, but a few do not. As Peterson points out, *Reader's Digest* and *Time* were among those begun on a shoestring, to say nothing of many very serviceable publications aimed at a limited audience.

And finally, even a very small magazine, whose market is too limited to permit newsstand distribution, can still reach into every corner of the United States through low postal rates which, for editorial matter, are uniform throughout the United States. This exceptionally far-sighted legislation, going back to 1879, made possible the first really national communications system in the United States and continues to be of the utmost importance. It is especially important to the magazine with little advertising (since the effective rates depend on the proportion of advertising matter) and to the specialized journal dependent on mail distribution. It has made it possible for the dweller in the most remote village in the United States to receive not only the popular weeklies and monthlies, but also the specialized technical journals—the medical or legal or agricultural journal—and even magazines of more limited cultural or scholarly interest, as conveniently and as cheaply as the resident of a great metropolis. The magazine is almost the only medium of communication in the country that has attained this relative uniformity of availability.

The technology and economic structure of magazine publishing are hence calculated to make possible an enormous flexibility in serving the varied needs of society, from magazines with mass circulation of millions to the highly specialized technical and learned journals and "little" magazines with a circulation in the hundreds, and to make any of them available quickly and cheaply to the most isolated person with the most specialized interests.

Magazines have responded well to the opportunities thus afforded, and it would be difficult today to find an informational or cultural need not reasonably adequately served insofar as it can be met within the limits of a magazine article. Not only are new magazines started to reflect the new range of interests of the period, but the content of almost every one of the popular magazines has shifted to devote less space to light entertainment and more to information. Such monthlies as *Harper's* and the *Atlantic* are almost solidly informational; the women's magazines now have articles on science and international relations as well as on cookery and child care; in such magazines as the *Saturday Evening Post* two-thirds or more of the content will now be solely informational, and the *Post* itself has indeed recently been carrying a really distinguished series of articles on new scientific and cultural trends; the *Scientific American* has become much more scientific while greatly increasing its circulation; and it is noteworthy that *Esquire,* which the Postmaster General only a few years ago sought to bar from second-class mailing privileges, has now become something of a journal of ideas.

In one respect, however, the economic organization of the industry does present some cause for concern, and that is in the case of the news magazines. Because the audience for general news does not, like the audience for news about chemical engineering or yachting or surgery, constitute a special market, a news magazine must depend on mass market advertisers and offer them a mass circulation. Experience has demonstrated that it is almost impossible to operate a news magazine profitably without a very large circulation. A magazine of incisive comment, diverging from established political points of view, has hard sledding, as evidenced by the *Reporter,* the *New Republic,* and the *National Review.* The difficulties of starting and sustaining a magazine in this field have brought it about that there are only three news magazines of large national circulation—*Time, Newsweek,* and *U.S. News and*

52

World Report—and a few others—like *Life* and the *Saturday Evening Post*—that editorialize a great deal. All of these, despite minor differences among them, reflect substantially a uniform point of view, that of the dominant business community to which their owners and advertisers and no doubt the majority of their subscribers belong.

This almost unchallenged dominance of a particular point of view in the news magazines is the more significant since the only other national news distribution is through the carefully neutral press services and news broadcasts and since the news magazines operate under no legal (as in the case of broadcasting stations) or traditional (as in the case of newspapers) limitation on editorializing in the news columns themselves. To have millions upon millions of readers view the events of the world regularly and persuasively presented, week after week, from a single political viewpoint is the more disturbing when that position uncritically reinforces—as at present—the point of view that is also dominant in government rather than challenging the philosophy in governmental control, as was very usefully the case in the last two administrations.

IX

Some of the same economic forces are operating in the case of newspapers as in the case of magazines, but there are important differences. It is difficult, except in the very largest cities, for newspapers to build up a special interest audience. Two or more competing newspapers hence offer the advertiser substantially similar audiences. To use both is frequently wastefully duplicative, and advertising support is likely to go to the paper with the larger or more "solid" circulation, thus creating a spiral effect that, as in the case of mass-circulation magazines, tends to push one of two originally nearly evenly matched competitors upward to prosperity and the other downward toward bankruptcy. This tendency is reinforced by the necessity of owning one's own printing facilities. Since these can represent a very heavy initial investment, the entry of new journals into competition is almost stopped. Only 123 new daily papers were founded between 1944 and 1953 and almost all of these were the first papers, or first daily papers, in new or very rapidly growing communities. To establish a newspaper successfully in competition with existing journals is very nearly impossible, and the attempt is now almost never made. As has been pointed out, the trend is in fact in the opposite direction. The number of cities with competing newspapers is falling rapidly and the trend is almost certain to continue. Even where competition continues, it is not often based on any very sharp diversity of political or economic views. The daily press, though not quite so unanimously, predominantly coincides in view with the national news magazines.

Moreover, the sharp competition for circulation, probably coupled with the increasing reliance of the public on magazines and broadcasts for national and international news, has meant that the newspapers have concentrated on circulation-building features little related to solid news. In most newspapers comic strips, contests, recipes, advice to the lovelorn columns, news of movie stars, horoscopes, and frequently trivial or sensational local news fill half or more of the 40 per cent or so of newsprint left over from advertising. In only a few cities of the United States is it possible to get any comprehensive coverage of foreign news, and many of the very largest cities would be missing from this list. Only a tiny handful of papers pretend to adequate news coverage of science or of education or religion except on a local basis. In only two cities are there separate book review sections.

54

X

Books share with magazines many economic attributes that make them especially serviceable in meeting the communication needs of the mid-twentieth century. Especially important among these is that the capital requirement for entering the publishing of books is even lower than in the case of magazines. It is not necessary to own production facilities; distribution by an established publisher can often be arranged; and specialized books can often be sold successfully by mail on the basis of a very modest investment in advertising in appropriate specialized journals. In consequence, there are several hundred book publishing firms, none of them achieving more than 5 per cent of the total market, and with numbers of new firms annually launched. Nor is it necessary to commit oneself to a continuing program of fixed size. An association or foundation or church group can bring out a book from time to time as it feels need to express its view on any particular problem without maintaining the overhead of a general publishing house.

Also important is the fact that a high proportion of the cost of any book depends on the number of copies distributed and a relatively low proportion, as compared with broadcasting, is a fixed initial cost. This means that a book can be profitably published for an audience infinitesimally small as compared with those of the mass media. What this "break-even" point is is a matter of considerable debate. It depends on the type of book and of publisher and on how overhead is allocated, but the figure probably generally lies between 5,000 and 7,500 copies for general trade publishers. University presses and others with low overheads have, of course, a much lower "break-even" point, as do commercial publishers with needed but specialized technical manuals that can be priced at a level that takes into account their anticipated small sale. In any event hundreds of books are published annually that sell under 2,500 copies, and that only over a period of months or years. This is to be compared with the concern recently expressed as to whether there was any possible way to keep going an excellent, if not most popular, television show which could do no better than a Sunday night audience of 8,000,-000 every week.

There have been complaints about the steady rise in the "break-even" point due to increased costs of labor and printing and paper, and it has risen a substantial but indeterminate amount. So too, however, has the potential market, and it is probably no more difficult for a given title to reach its break-even point today than at the beginning of the century. Certainly a great many more books of more specialized kinds are being published, though it is true that many of the scholarly books, and even much of the poetry, that were brought out a generation ago by general publishers must now be issued by university presses. So far as society is concerned, however, they can still be published. For even smaller audiences, the book format, if not always the trade distribution mechanisms, can be used for works offset from typed copy, which can be issued for a few hundred readers.

It is of a further enormous advantage that this audience does not have to be brought together at one time, as for a broadcast, or be found in one locality, as for a newspaper or local radio or television station, or be reassembled weekly or monthly as for a magazine. In consequence, books can be published for the most limited, specialized, and minority audiences of all the media of communications.

Books differ from magazines, of course, in deriving none of their revenue from advertising. Though this forces a higher price for the product, it does relieve an editor of the necessity of considering whether any given publication will assemble the sort of audience that would make a homogeneous market for a given class of products, and hence places the communications service of

56

books entirely at the service of the reader and his interests rather than the advertiser and his.

The fact that the book industry pays an author by means of a royalty per copy sold rather than on a flat fee or salary basis also has beneficial consequences. The writer in most media, like broadcasting or films or newspapers and news magazines, is an employee, hired to create a predetermined product on assignment with his work belonging to the employer and subject to revision by him. Even in the case of magazines with signed articles, the writer's work is selected because in the editor's judgment it will be of interest to an audience of the size and kind reached by the magazine. Only in books is the author an independent partner in the enterprise, served by rather than serving the publisher. If he has something he wants to say badly enough, even to a small audience, he can go ahead, venturing the small return.

The format of the book also has a social utility. Its length makes possible the extended and comprehensive discussion of subjects in a way that can be undertaken in no other medium. The fact that it requires no devices such as screens, projectors or receiving sets for its use means that it can be read privately, anywhere and at any time. Even more important is the fact that its format lends itself to the assembly of books in collections—as in bookstores or public or private libraries—in which the reader has his free choice at one moment among thousands or even tens or hundreds of thousands of communications, covering almost every conceivable subject from varied points of view—a choice never offered in such diversity and richness by other media. On the other hand, the physical requirements of book preparation, production, and distribution mean that it is very slow as a reportorial device. Broadcasts, newspapers, magazines and scholarly and technical journals are far faster in reporting news of all kinds, not only of spot events but also of general educational or scientific developments.

In other respects books suffer from some serious disadvantages. The fact that each book must be "sold" separately means that an extraordinarily heavy burden is placed on the introduction of new writers. Most novels by new writers are published at a substantial loss to the publisher and find only a very limited readership. A new writer will be more easily published and will find a wider audience as the writer of a short story for a magazine than as the author of a novel, because the magazine has an already established and in part contracted for audience to which it can introduce his work.

The cost of distributing all books, and not only those by new authors, is high. The very abundance of books—with the 13,000 or so new ones every year, the 125,000 in print and the many hundreds of thousands out of print but handled by second-hand stores—and the absence (except for book-clubs) of any automatic method of putting them in readers' hands mean that a formidable operation is necessary simply to keep track of this enormous inventory, to publicize new books, and to distribute them in little trickles through the thousands of communities in the United States. The physical costs of distribution are further increased by the fact that the postal rate on books is several times higher than that on the editorial matter in magazines. Well over half the total cost of a book goes not to compensate its author or manufacturer or publisher, but simply to pay the costs of letting the reader know about it and of getting it from the bindery into his hands.

Not only is the distribution system expensive, it is pitifully ineffective. To serve a population of over 180,000,000 persons in the United States, there are only about 1,500 bookstores worthy of the name even by a rather generous definition. Almost all of these are in cities of 50,000 or larger, and there are a good many cities even of that size without an adequate bookstore. Most bookstores are not in high-traffic locations and most of them are regularly

58

patronized by only a tiny fragment of the population, probably less than 1 per cent.

Nor are there effective means of simply letting people know what is available. Even the most extensive review medium, the *Library Journal,* reviews less than 40 per cent of the books published. The largest medium aimed at the general public, *The New York Times Book Review,* reviews about 20 per cent. In most newspapers with any book reviews (a small minority) only 1 per cent or 2 per cent will be covered. In the face of the enormous burden of advertising thousands of new titles annually, publishers can rarely afford to advertise in national media or in newspapers outside a relatively few cities. The great majority of books made available annually pass in silence, entirely unknown to the general public.

The inadequacy of bookstores as a channel of distribution for books has led to the increasing use of other means—notably door-to-door sales, book clubs, distribution of paperbound books through magazine channels, and direct mail sales. About a fourth of the dollar volume of book sales in the United States are "subscription," i.e., door-to-door sales, but these are made up of expensive sets, almost entirely encyclopedias. Book clubs and paperbound sales through magazine wholesalers now make up over half of all sales of books other than textbooks, and are the means through which most Americans acquire books. They have overcome the numerical and geographic limitations of the bookstore, making books available everywhere. More importantly, by laying books across his path at the station, the airport, the drug store, the five-and-ten, the supermarket, the hotel lobby and the kiosk and by bringing books into his home unless he takes specific action to cancel an order, the magazine wholesaler and the book club have overcome the inertia that inhibited one's making a special trip to a bookstore and selecting a particular book. And they have made books much cheaper.

But these values have been achieved at a cost. The lower prices and the greater efficiency of these methods of book distribution come not primarily from economies in manufacture, though these are important, but from curtailing the cost of offering the reader a choice. The variety and quality of books in print in mass-distributed paper editions and the range of book-club offerings have greatly increased; but only a small percentage of books published, and only those of rather general interest, can be distributed at all in this way. And it is of the essence of the economics of both schemes that the number of choices on the newsstand at any one time, or the books offered in any one month by any one book club to which the reader belongs, are severely and necessarily limited. Each of these methods of distribution greatly enlarges the flow of books to the American people; neither is a substitute for the bookstore in terms of offering to the reader the whole range of intellectual and informational resources the book offers.[4]

There is, of course, the remaining alternative of sales by mail. It is possible for anyone anywhere with diligence and patience to get any book he wants. But in practice, mail sales are effective in distributing only two kinds of books: the potentially very popular book that is bought usually for other purposes than the pleasure of reading and finds its market outside the regular book-buyers (how-to-do-it books and popular medical books are examples) and books for specialized professional audiences too thinly scattered to be effectively served by bookstore distribution but easily reached through mailing lists based on their professional groupings or advertisements in professional journals.

The consequence of this pattern of book distribution is that the enormously rich and varied resources of books are realistically available through commercial channels only to a very small and

[4] Mass-distributed paperbound books are now being sold in an increasing number of bookstores, some of which, especially in larger cities, are able to offer a range of several hundred or even several thousand titles.

60

favored fraction of the residents of rather large cities and university communities. Realizing perhaps both the extraordinary social utility of books as a medium of communication and the severe limitations imposed by their distribution system, the state has intervened more directly than in the case of any of the other media to supplement the available distribution facilities. This has been done through a network of public libraries.

In addition to the public library system as a means of carrying books to the general public, school and college libraries provide for their special availability as needed in education; and university libraries, the largest public libraries, and libraries of major corporations, research institutions, and governmental agencies have accumulated collections needed for research.

Though all of these forms of library service were greatly improved and extended in the preceding generation, there continue to be grave weaknesses. There remain major problems of accumulating, and more particularly of organizing and controlling, the vast bodies of materials needed for the range and depth of contemporary research. Though all colleges and most high schools have "libraries," three-fourths of elementary schools have none. And a minority of college, high school, or elementary school libraries are adequate to meet the needs of enlarged enrollments and expanding curricula. There is the gravest reason in particular to fear that the college library resources of the country will be wholly inadequate to meet the flood of students that is expected to double college enrollment in the coming 10 or 15 years. And in only a few favored institutions are the library resources capable of supporting the kind of instruction the times seem to call for, in which every student needs to have an abundant and individualized opportunity for independent learning and development.

But quantitatively the most serious inadequacies are in the public library field. In 1955-56 there were 6,249 public library systems that responded to Office of Education questionnaires.

These served a total population of 117,607,000, leaving a total population of 45,000,000 with no public library service except as it may have been given by the few hundred institutions too small or indifferent to have been included in the Office of Education statistics. Probably 30,000,000 were totally without library service and entirely dependent on commercial sources. Tens of millions of others were served by libraries so small as to offer only a handful of books out of the range of resources available.

Probably half the total population of the country at mid-century have no library service, or library service so poor as to offer no realistic access to the national resources of books. This half the country is, almost without exception, also totally unserved by bookstores and ill-served by paperbound books and book clubs. For most of the tens of millions of Americans on farms and in villages and very small towns, especially in the poorer regions of the country, the book hardly exists as a realistic means of communication.

It is probably a sound estimate that if one picks at random from the publishers' lists of a year ago any informative book not a best-seller but of solid substance and independent viewpoint, the odds are that in three-fourths of the counties of the U.S. there is no copy in any school or home or bookstore or library, and the book has never been reviewed or mentioned in any newspaper published in those counties or in any broadcast heard there or even in any magazine widely read there.

Chapter III *The Future*

American society has created a communications system unparalleled in its magnitude. Its members have more television sets and consume more newsprint than all the rest of the world together. The number and diversity of its magazines and the size of their circulation are nowhere else approached. Its research libraries are the largest and (with the possible exception of Russia) its public libraries, for all their inadequacy, are the most numerous. Contrary to the general impression, it leads almost all nations in the per capita production of books. The daily flow of communication to its citizens is certainly the largest in history. And it is a free flow, not under governmental control and probably less restricted by censorship than anywhere else in the world.

And yet there is deep social dissatisfaction with the state of the communications system. The banality and emptiness of most broadcasts and films, the "slickness" of magazines, the political bias of newspapers and news magazines, the cultural and political conformity of the mass media, sex and violence in books, films, and broadcasts, illiteracy and superficiality in cultural life—all are the subject of thoughtful and continuous complaint. To what degree is the communications system actually inadequate, and what needs to be done about it?

II

An objective appraisal would probably suggest four major weaknesses:

1. The system of recording and organizing advanced knowledge is not adequate to the current flood.

2. Knowledge is not widely enough spread. The mass of the citizenry is neither well enough trained to meet new occupational demands nor well enough informed as citizens.

3. The communications system has a built-in tendency to reinforce existing cultural interests and political views and is unreceptive to novelty and change.

4. The banality, tastelessness, and sensationalism of much of its content cheapens values and confuses purposes, rather than strengthening and clarifying them.

The first of these weaknesses, since it does not involve mass communications, deserves a somewhat separate treatment that cannot be adequately given within the confines of this study. Suffice it to say that the conventional methods of publishing the results of scientific research in journals and in books, and of organizing their content through bibliographies, catalogs, and indexes is breaking down under the flood of knowledge. There are not enough journals and they are not published fast enough to keep up with new research. The standard bibliographical tools are being overwhelmed or are becoming impossibly large, expensive, and slow. The bulk of the *Union List of Serials*, for example, has expanded geometrically with each edition.

The cataloging within each major research library is in more or less continual crisis, and is kept in balance only by abandoning the effort effectively to organize hugh masses of research material. A somewhat similar problem exists with regard to the acute need to strengthen our national resources of research materials from less known foreign areas, particularly Eastern Europe, Asia, and

64

the Middle East. Uncoordinated acquisitions and the lack of sufficient cataloging staffs able to use the languages concerned, create a chaotic situation.

There is an acute awareness of particular segments of this problem, and various efforts to deal with certain of its aspects are under way. Each of the major scientific disciplines knows something of its own problem, and many of them are making individual efforts toward solutions. There are committees of the various library associations to deal with such specific problems as the *Union List of Serials,* microcards, or the National Union Catalog, or with codes for the cataloging of less used materials. Each individual research library is endeavoring to cope with its own cataloging arrearages.

Two programs to deal with the problem have a more general scope. The National Science Foundation has a major responsibility for dealing with the recording, organization, and dissemination of scientific information, particularly in fields relevant to the national security, and has substantial funds to devote to the purpose. And the Ford Foundation created in 1955 the Council on Library Resources with an endowment of $5,000,000 and the possibility of further grants to deal with the whole problem of library resources for research. Both of these agencies have attacked the problem with energy, and on the whole one can be optimistic about the progress likely to be made.

Three aspects of the whole problem of the documentation of knowledge have not yet been generally faced, however. One is that the basic difficulties are not to be overcome with mechanical devices. Indeed the problems of organizing human knowledge that so press upon us, and threaten to drown further scientific progress in oceans of print are intellectual, not mechanical or electronic, in nature. The patterns of subject analysis used in most scholarly libraries and bibliographical tools were developed over a half century ago. Our need may well be for the creation of radically new subject approaches—new ways of fitting tags or handles to all the overflowing pieces of knowledge we must manipulate; an even more certain need is for far larger manpower resources to do the subject analysis—to fit the handles. If we can achieve these, our problem from then on will be easily soluble, whether by alphabetized handwritten slips or the pulsing transistors of a giant brain.

A second is that no one institution or group of federal institutions alone can meet the full national need for accumulating and organizing research materials. Our national needs can be met only if the total resources of all research institutions—in terms both of holdings and of capacity for cataloging and organizing materials—are considered as a single interlinked national resource. If there were far more cooperative acquisitions and cataloging and bibliographical effort, the burden on each institution would be smaller, and the effectiveness of the total network of resources would be greater. But needs for cooperative action come at a time when every research institution is overwhelmed with work imperatively needed to get its own holdings in order and serve its immediate constituents. There is a serious need for continuing funds to support activities in institutions throughout the country that contribute primarily to national rather than local needs. Federal funds, except for some National Science Foundation projects, rarely go to such purposes; and foundation grants are too exclusively restricted to experimental as opposed to operational needs.

The third is that the problems, though perhaps most acutely felt in science and technology, are by no means confined to those fields. Indeed, over the long run, the problems of assembling and organizing adequate bodies of documentation in the social sciences, especially with reference to the Slavic, Middle Eastern and Asian areas, may well prove to be even more difficult and important.

66

What is especially needed now is a responsible body, supported by either federal or foundation funds, able to make a continuing critical review of the total national resources of research documentation in terms of library holdings, cataloging and bibliographical needs, and means of disseminating information and also in terms of the adequacy of that total assemblage of resources to meet *national* needs. Such a body will need means to help finance additional activities it finds necessary. In the absence of such a body, only piecemeal and inadequate steps are likely, dealing with individual problems more or less in isolation.

III

The consequences of the second major weakness— the failure of the communications system to spread knowledge deeply or widely enough—are painfully and increasingly apparent. The Soviet gains upon the United States in many areas of science and technology have shocked Americans into a long overdue concern for the state of knowledge. This is usually expressed, and with some justification, as an attack on the superficial and undemanding character of much of American education. But the formal educational system alone certainly cannot bear the whole burden of maintaining the scientific and technical proficiency of the people. Its contact with students extends at most to their early twenties, at which point a lifetime of rapid technological change still lies ahead of them. It can equip its students with little more than the ability to understand new developments, and a drive to keep themselves informed. The subsequent development of their knowledge depends on the communications system and the opportunities it affords—the availability of scientific and technical books and journals and the use of the mass media for continuing training and retraining in these fields.

Much the same thing is true of occupational skills in general.

It has been pointed out that we are in the midst of perhaps the largest series of shifts in employment in history. Hundreds of thousands of farmers a year are being moved into urban employment. Mechanical power has already displaced the man who brought only his muscles to his work—the digger of ditches, the turner of furrows, the bearer of burdens. Routine skills, both mechanical and clerical, are now in the process of similar replacement by automated machines. The massive impact of these changes has not yet been fully felt because of high employment in other sectors of the economy and because of demographic peculiarities that make the present working population an unusually small proportion of the total population. But soon we shall feel it heavily. Meanwhile, the same series of changes is creating a continuing and unfilled demand for professional men and women, administrators, planners, and skilled technicians. To produce beginners in these highly trained fields is, of course, the responsibility of the schools and universities. But it is characteristic of all the professional and occupational skills now in demand that a constant and immediate adjustment to new situations and an ability to make use of new knowledge are indispensable. For this the professional man and the trained worker in general need a larger access to current knowledge than they now typically have; and this need will continue to grow rapidly.

But our ignorance is most evident and most dangerous in the field of public affairs. With a depressing regularity, whenever one of the public opinion polls asks the views of a large cross-section of Americans about any issue more complex than whom they plan to vote for as President, a very large percentage will never even have heard of the issue being debated. And if inquiry were made as to the depth and quantity of knowledge on any of these issues, the result would be even more depressing. Because of the more instant mobilization of public opinion and its more effective

68

expression to which I referred in the first of these talks, we have admitted far more people than ever before to a real voice in government, expressed not merely in the elections at which so many more now vote, but in the direct impact of their views on individual issues. We have done so at a time when meaningful participation in government requires knowledge outside our normal spheres of experience to a degree so much greater than in earlier generations as to pose the problem of effective democracy in new terms. Yet we have by no means correspondingly extended realistic access to the information needed for that participation.

The ignorance of which I speak is, of course, only relative. The citizenry at large is better educated and better informed on current issues than ever before, and a larger freight of information goes out through the communications system than ever before. But it is relative to a need for competent, trained, thoughtful, and informed citizens of an almost desperate degree. The functional illiteracy of most Americans today is a far graver menace to our future than was the actual illiteracy of a century or more ago.

What we confront, of course, is that the traditional bearers of complex and extensive bodies of information—books, learned and technical journals, and the higher level magazines—have remained largely confined in their circulation to their traditional and relatively restricted audiences at a time when the need for the information in them has become much broader. And the media that have achieved the broader circulation—the truly mass media —have with minor exceptions failed to undertake this responsibility. Our imperiling ignorance is the consequence on the one hand of the non-existent bookstores and the impoverished libraries, and on the other of the empty hours of Westerns and soap opera that have squandered so much of the tremendous potentialities of the newer media.

IV

Yet more serious, I believe, is the overemphasis of predominant or majority views and interests that is "built into" the communications system. We have seen that the very technology of films and especially of broadcasting is such that their efficiency can be realized only when they are reaching very large audiences. This is a constant factor that is just as present in the BBC as in the advertising-supported networks of the United States. This technological fact predisposes all the mass media to conform to an already widely accepted taste. It also makes it very difficult for a novel point of view or a just emerging problem to gain access to network broadcasts or other mass components of the communications system. Let me make it clear once more that I am not talking about the ability of each of two conflicting points of view to get on the air so long as each is a well-recognized point of view about a controversy that already commands attention. It is rather the subject or point of view in which people are not yet interested, but ought to be, that finds understandable difficulty in gaining access to the mass media.

This is not surprising and it would perhaps not even be regrettable if it were not for the dominant position in communication that the mass media hold. If there were a sufficient variety in the channels of communication daily reaching people, there would be little cause for concern in the fact that the channels best adapted technologically for mass audiences should be almost entirely filled with material of an assured mass interest. The fact is, however, that the mass media make up the overwhelming majority of communication reception by the overwhelming majority of people, certainly on matters outside their spheres of immediate interest. (That is, the doctor reads medical journals for his professional information, but relies on *Time* and TV for his political impressions.) Hence there is an overwhelming ten-

70

dency to reinforce whatever is already strongest and to weaken through neglect whatever does not already command mass attention.

This tendency is greatly magnified by the fact that the cost of most of the daily mass communications received by Americans is borne by advertisers. As we have pointed out earlier, it is this fact, coupled with the large capital investment for printing plants, that has nearly eliminated newspaper competition in the United States. The desire of the advertiser to reach the largest possible audience with his sales message greatly reinforces the natural propensity of the mass media to concentrate solely on mass audiences. This is especially true in the case of broadcasting, which cannot effectively reach the specialized markets served by magazines and hence must attract mass advertisers that in turn seek mass assemblages of general consumers as an audience. Through the mechanism described earlier the drive toward the "big" audience, which is perhaps the inevitable consequence of the technology of the mass media, is transformed into a constant drive for the "biggest" audience by the needs of advertisers.

More serious yet is the fact that in broadcasting the advertiser determines the content of the program he sponsors. He desires not only a very big audience, but an audience that has not been offended or depressed or startled or shocked or stimulated to resentment or rejection that might unconsciously be attached to the advertised product. As we have pointed out, he wants rather a program that is compatible with the audience's views and interests and will achieve with the audience those reactions of approval and credibility that attach to a communication that confirms one's already established positions.

For all of these reasons the mass components of our communications system, which overwhelmingly predominate in the attention of the public, echo what already is. One fears malign purposes at the center of the communications web, "hidden persuaders" who seek to transform us surreptitiously, political propagandists—more subtle Goebbelses—who will insidiously corrupt our independence. Our danger is, however, quite different. The vast mechanism of communication which so surrounds us and fills our hours and creates for us the meaning of the world beyond our daily round is rather painstakingly devoted, through polls and ratings and surveys and tests, to finding out just what we are like now, what interests us, what our tastes are, what our prejudices are, and then holding up for us a vast and rose-tinted mirror. It is not Big Brother that speaks from the screen; it is the homogenized image of ourselves, the same image that is reflected from the daily press and the pages of the news magazine.

In any massive communications system in which the variety of simultaneous communications is necessarily limited, some means of deciding the content carried by the system must be adopted. A political autocracy may give the listeners a fare that shapes them to its will, as in Russia; a minority of cultural leaders, as in Britain, may try to aim the programs at a cultural pitch just enough higher than the average taste to exercise the maximum lift upon that taste—high enough to elevate the audience but not so high as to lose it; or the system may seek only to give the audience what it wants. We have chosen the third, and reinforced it with a form of advertising support that relentlessly defines "audience" in the largest numbers and relentlessly defines its interests in the least challenging and controversial terms. The consequence is to press majority toward unanimity and to reinforce existing tastes and views with their own constant and amplified echo.

Of course this is not always and uniformly true. One thinks, for example, of the recent series in *Life* on abstract expressionist art, which could hardly be in sharper conflict with what is doubtless the dominant taste of *Life* readers, or the *Saturday Evening Post's* remarkable series of articles on contemporary thought and ideas by intellectual leaders. Television too, has its examples,

72

though one is somewhat driven to thinking of local programs, like New York's independent station's *Open End* or subsidized programs like *Omnibus* in its early days.

But there can be no question that the unconscious and inevitable influence of the communications system operates powerfully and pervasively toward fixing a relatively unchallenged consensus around the dominant view. This was set forth with painful vividness by a news columnist who had accompanied both Mr. Nixon and Mr. Khrushchev on their visits to each other's countries. Noting the warmth of Nixon's reception by ordinary Russians and the coldness and hostility of the popular attitude in this country toward Khrushchev, he pointed out that the free press of the United States had done a much more effective job of creating an unrelievedly black image in this country of Russian leadership than had the governmentally controlled Soviet press after decades of effort in creating a uniformly bad impression of American leaders among the Russian people. (No doubt, of course, the facts made their job easier!) Indeed it would probably be harder to find favorable reference to any part of the activities of the Russian or Communist Chinese governments in the popular media of the United States than it would be to find comparable references to the United States in Russian newspapers or broadcasts.

This tendency is powerfully aided by two factors. One is that broadcasts have only a limited time to deal with any subject. On telecasts much of that limited time is devoted to pictorial presentation, which, though it adds greatly to the vividness of any statement, can be effective only if very simple. It is therefore easiest for broadcasts, and particularly for television, to present subjects in highly simplified, not to say superficial, form. The conceptions of issues built up by television, and to a large degree by radio and the popular press, hence tend to cluster around certain unqualified "polar" positions. The reality of all the most

critical problems with which we are engaged is almost unbelievably complex. Perhaps the greatest weakness in our handling
of them has been an ignorance—or an ignoring—of that complexity. A China policy has been reduced to "support Chiang and
refuse to recognize Communist China." A Middle East policy has
been reduced to "resist Communist aggression"—the least, probably, of all the threats to that unhappy region. We send arms to
Iraq and back a regional alliance against aggression, thinking of
these as purely anti-Communist measures, apparently quite without anticipating the regional repercussions within the Middle
East, where these moves had profound and probably undesirable
consequences for the internal balance of power. It is suggested
that our response to all the infinitely varied possibilities and
degrees of aggression against us be simplified to the one alternative of submission or a mutually suicidal massive retaliation.

These are, of course, policies of men whose image of the international situation is by no means dependent on the mass media;
but they are policies supported by, and in a sense demanded by,
a public trained to conceive of issues in simplistic terms. Public
reaction to the Korean War demonstrates the problem. As long
as this was a simple answer—"Fight back"—to a simple problem—
"the Communists are attacking"—our resistance commanded en-
thusiastic popular support. As soon as our role became a complex
and realistically limited response to a complex and extremely
dangerous situation, it was totally rejected by the American
people, even though without bringing on a general war it was
successful in ending open Communist aggression, not only for
then but for a decade thereafter. Similarly, during World War
II, in the face of the over-simplified picture presented by the
Government and the mass media of the Russians as staunch allies,
and of the over-simplified concept of the war as a purely military
operation, it was impossible to adopt more complex and qualified
policies that, at the expense of prolonging the war somewhat,

74

might have achieved a better political and military position vis-a-vis the Russians at its close. The falsely simple pictures of the world and its problems are so deeply and effectively planted by the mass media, and public response to those over-simplifications is made so vigorous, that public policy itself becomes shaped in those terms.

The other factor reinforcing the tendency toward over-simplified uniformity is that with respect to all the issues of most vital importance to us, the Government is almost the only source of detailed information, much of which is classified and to be released or withheld at the Government's discretion. This is particularly true of matters relating to the use of atomic energy. Almost all the facts relevant to the wisdom of continuing bomb-testing, for example—both its need and its dangers—are only to be had at the Government's hands. So also with the data needed to appraise our missile policy, or the adequacy of our research program in military fields. It is almost equally true in foreign relations, in which the Government's sources of information are obviously vastly superior to any others. Even the scientific research in areas relevant to national policy and a good part of the research in foreign affairs and social sciences that is carried on in the universities is Government supported and controlled. This situation will certainly continue and the areas of knowledge dominated by the Government are likely to grow.

When the power to govern is so linked with control over the information needed to appraise the acts of government, it is of the utmost importance that the communications process itself subject the flow of data to the maximum independent criticism. We need—we deeply need—to have our information in these sensitive areas reach us through a variety in channels in which it has been appraised, tested, commented on from as many points of view as possible. It will be fatal to the ends of government itself if we are reduced to the blind following of government policy because the only view of issues we have is one uncritically shaped for us by the communications system from the materials provided by the Government. Yet, as we have seen, it is the almost inescapable propensity of the communications system as it is now organized to echo and reinforce the dominant position.

A further re-inforcement comes from the fact that the owners of newspapers, magazines and broadcasting media and the advertisers with whom they are sympathetically related are for the most part businessmen of wealth reflecting with near, though not absolute unanimity, a common general view of most aspects of affairs, a view which in recent years has coincided rather closely with that of the Administration. Though Federal Communications Commission rulings limit the overt expression of owner's views in broadcasts, there is no such limitation on the press, either on newspapers or on news magazines, which have been overwhelmingly Republican in party politics for the last twenty years and in general conservative on most issues.

When the great issue of the time is whether we shall be able to achieve a sufficiently rapid social adaptation to accommodate to the revolutionary changes introduced by science and technology, the weight of the communications system—not by deliberate choice, but by its structure—is to smother the novelty of thought that might introduce swift, orderly, and constructive change, and instead to reinforce what is. Imperial Rome and Egypt, Charles I and George III and Louis XVI and Nicholas II exemplify rigidity in the face of needed change. May the United States profit by their example.

V

A final weakness is that the overwhelmingly dominant use of the new communications resources developed in this century—films, radio, and television—has been to convey not in-

76

formation or opinions or works of art created because the composer or author has something to say, but rather entertainment created to formula because something has to be produced to occupy the theater screens and the broadcast channels. This sort of contrived entertainment has, of course, always existed, but not until our century have there been physical means to disseminate it so widely. That perhaps 10 per cent of the waking hours of the average American is now devoted to the passive reception of this "kitsch," as commercial entertainment has come to be called, is a novel phenomenon of our times. There has never been anything quite like it, and its consequences are unpredictable.

There has been a special concern not merely that so much of the steady entertainment is empty and meretricious, but that so much of it is concerned with sex and violence and sentimentality. I do not think, however, that the issue is really over sex and violence in themselves. The *Gunfight at the O.K. Corral* has nothing on the final scene of *Hamlet* for violence, and *Hamlet* has incest, insanity, poisoning and treason thrown in for good measure. Many of the greatest masterpieces of literature and drama confront the sexual passions and tragedies of man more nakedly than any film or tawdry publication today. It is rather that sex and violence are dissociated from the human realities that give them meaning and made gimmicks to spice up an advertisement or catch attention at a newsstand. This is another consequence of the use of many of our major resources for communication not as a link between persons with something to say and an audience with a cause to listen, but rather as a marketing device, with the needs of marketing rather than the creative impulses of authors or the needs of listeners as the determinant of content.

I am not an alarmist about the question of "kitsch." I suspect that its emptiness expresses rather than creates the moral vacuity of society about which we are concerned. But certainly in a time in which one of our most critical needs is a re-founding of values, there is little in the daily flow of communication that will help. Even most of the religious programs on the air, the Biblical films, and the popular religious writings are more often than not a sentimental evasion rather than a confrontation of the philosophical and value problems of the mid-twentieth century.

VI

We have the problem of measuring the efficiency of our communications system and exploring what we can do to improve it. The developments in communication in this generation have been hailed as vastly increasing that efficiency. And so they have, if we measure efficiency from the point of view of the producer of communication. Ten million people can be reached much more surely, far more cheaply, and incomparably more quickly by a broadcast than by the use of print. It has been said that more people saw *Hamlet* in one television performance than had ever seen it in all the theatrical performances of more than three centuries. In one hour's broadcast a presidential candidate can reach more people with a statement of his views than he ever could hope to see face-to-face even in months of whistle-stopping. A manufacturer can have an audience of tens of millions assembled to hear an advertisement of his product at one time. A teacher has vivid new teaching materials at her command. A government that wants people to buy defense bonds or enlist in the Air Force or avoid forest fires—or for that matter a government that wants people to hate Jews or adopt atheism or forego butter for guns—has a much more efficient means of stimulus and persuasion at hand. Whoever has a message to convey and can get access to the newer media can convey it more widely and quickly and to a mass audience more cheaply than ever before.

This sort of efficiency has positive social values. The progres-

78

sively more complete and effective mobilization of national effort in the Revolutionary War, the Civil War, and the First and Second World Wars reflects the progressively greater efficiency of the communications system. Without the same sort of efficiency, a national economy so integrated and complex as ours simply could not hang together.

Yet this efficiency is not the same thing as efficiency measured from the point of view of the consumer of communication. His choice of the newer media, unless he lives in a very large city, is likely on any evening to be confined to two television programs and a half a dozen on radio and perhaps three or four films. If his desires are more specific than for casual entertainment or daily news he almost certainly will be frustrated. For the user who wants to become a better lathe operator, or keep abreast of new medical techniques, or find out something about antique furniture or the government of Pakistan, or find out for himself what the dangers of atomic radiation are or hear a particular Mozart concerto, or see or read again an Ibsen play, or indeed gratify any curiosity or desire that is personal and individual to him, the mass media are exceptionally inefficient. Even an impoverished small-town library, for all its painful lacks, is likely to serve him better.

The values of a free society by and large lie on the side of the values of the individual consumer of communication rather than on the side of the values of the producers of communication. What we need is a communications system that gives the individual consumer the greatest resources to satisfy his needs for information and enrichment, and that strengthens his capacity to achieve personal development and autonomy of judgment. We need a communications system whose built-in "lean" is toward increasing the range of information and of different sources of opinion and of different cultural experiences that are simultaneously and conveniently available to each user rather than a system whose "lean" is rather toward increasing the size of the audience simultaneously and conveniently available to one speaker.

The questions of public policy involved in seeking such a communications system are rarely seen as a whole. They come up in bits and pieces, in a debate on postal rates, or in discussions of the FCC's licensing procedure, or in antitrust suits against the film industry, or in censorship actions, or in measures for library support. To evolve a unified communications policy would require extended and careful study of many exceedingly complex and technical questions and is obviously far beyond the scope of this or any series of lectures. A glance at the enormous mass of Congressional hearings on the one question of station-network relationships in broadcasting will suggest how exceedingly complicated are some of the problems involved. But perhaps we can sketch some of the objectives that ought to be sought in such a policy and some of its possible components.

VII

The object of public policy in communications ought to be to open the way to diversity in serving the public's diverse needs. In some ways this is a negative and certainly a modest policy. It will surely not revolutionize the content of the mass media with Shakespeare and Mozart and science lectures as daily fare. For better or for worse, I hold to the view that people ought to have what they want, even if what most of them want most of the time is superficial, empty, or distasteful. I do not like my listening or viewing or reading dictated by those who want to improve my mind and broaden my culture any more than by those who want to improve my morals and safeguard me from political error.

But people are different and want different things, and when we say that the communications system should give them what

80

they want, it means that *all* the different audiences should, as nearly as practicable, get what they want—including those that *do* want Shakespeare or Mozart or science lectures—or to know what is going on in Africa or how to grow begonias or how the Taft-Hartley Act works. Magazines, particularly the more specialized ones, and books can now serve this need fairly well—not from any virtue on the part of their publishers but because of the way their economics and technology work. But they do not reach enough people. Broadcasting reaches enough people but it is hampered, almost crippled, by its present technology and economics in serving any but the largest and lowest-common-denominator audiences. So part of the problem is to spread print wider, and part of it is to introduce more diversity into broadcasting.

VIII

The public prints—though notably not the airwaves—have been filled with recent suggestions for improving broadcasting, brought to something of a climax by the quiz-show scandals. Walter Lippmann and others have proposed that a whole network be supported by the government or by foundations for high-level broadcasting dissociated from advertisers. Other suggestions widely made include divorcing advertisers from matters of program content and modifying the relations between networks and affiliated stations. I do not believe that any of these will solve the problem.

No foundation or group of foundations could afford to sustain the regular operating cost of a TV network, and even if one could, I suspect that the foundation's insistence on non-controversiality would prove as deadening as the advertiser's. Nor do I believe that the United States government can safely be entrusted with the support of a broadcasting network, even though it were insulated from the conduct of political affairs by such a device as a public corporation along the lines of the BBC. Our traditions are different from those of the British; in particular our ways of appropriating funds are different. It would be inevitable that annually when the television authority—or whatever we might call it—came up for its appropriation, program content would receive a vigorous Congressional scrutiny. Nothing in our experience with other Government adventures into mass communication suggests that creative independence could be maintained. Diversity and novelty would be far harder to achieve than under almost any form of private operation. And in any event, it is of the utmost importance to separate the communications system as far as possible from the other seats of power in our society.

The now widely supported idea that advertisers should have nothing to do with program content, but merely buy time for commercials as they now buy space for advertisements in a magazine or newspaper, is appealing because of that analogy. It is the rule in British commercial television, and I believe that it would be desirable here as far as it goes. Certainly if the sponsor did not fear his product would be held responsible by viewers for anything they disliked in a program, we might have more daring and original programming and more candor in dealing with controversial subjects. But too much cannot be expected from this proposed reform. As we have pointed out, conditions in broadcasting are quite different from those in magazines and newspapers. The circulation of the publication is guaranteed and does not depend on the editorial content adjacent to any given advertisement. Readers can look through the advertisements for what they want, regardless of the adjoining content, which they may read at another time. And there is nothing to identify an advertiser with any given editorial item. In broadcasting, in contrast, the audience for a commercial depends entirely on how large an audience is "pulled" by the concurrent program, and they come to the commercial "conditioned" by the program. The advertiser hence

82

cannot physically be dissociated from program content to the degree possible in publications. He has a vital interest in the program surrounding his commercial, and that interest will find expression regardless of regulations. The station or network anxious to attract advertisers, though it may have full responsibility for programming, is likely to discharge that responsibility in the closest consultation with the sponsor or potential sponsor.

The network problem is even more complicated. Networks are now allowed to own up to five VHF stations and two UHF stations outright, and those are of course in the largest cities. With its other stations, which are independently owned, the network may have contracts giving it the option to buy time at specified hours, usually the prime evening hours. These arrangements enable the network to guarantee a sponsor exposure of his program in all principal market areas and also assure it enough business to maintain its very expensive network of leased cables for transmitting programs to affiliated stations. On the other hand, local affiliates are denied the opportunity to put on their own shows at those hours and sell time directly to local or national advertisers. Producers of syndicated series on film have particularly objected to being barred from the network-owned stations and during most prime hours from the affiliates. The situation is quite similar to the earlier movie problem of producer-owned theaters. The government now has the matter under study from an antitrust point of view.

There is much to be said, as in the motion picture case, for breaking up this sort of arrangement and compelling the networks to sell their shows to local stations on a competitive basis. But there are formidable technical problems relating to the maintenance of transmission lines; and from the programming quality point of view, weakening the networks might well prove to be undesirable. The more constructive answer, I believe, is to increase the number of independent local stations.

This is indeed the most important issue of all in the broadcasting field. There is no real hope for an effective representation of the tastes and interests of even quite large minorities without a great many more stations. This would be easily possible if the entire UHF spectrum were used. The difficulty is that broadcasts in those frequencies cannot be received by present TV sets without adapters. The few educational stations assigned UHF channels have been almost total failures because local viewers were not prepared to buy adapters; and there is little commercial interest in the channels for the same reason. I believe the only answer is to shift all televising to UHF, at least in areas without six or seven available VHF channels. This would occasion a great expense for adapters and would cause a real outcry among television set owners. But the future is a lot longer than the present, and we are setting the patterns of our communications for indefinite decades to come. The longer we postpone, the more difficult and costly the change. This action seems to me the basis of most other reforms in broadcasting.

The second necessary step is a more adequate support of educational television and radio stations. Neither states nor cities nor the federal government have faced up to this problem. Channels have been reserved but only a minority are in use, and there is hardly an educational station that is not stumbling along with insufficient funds and amateurish and under-financed programming. Even New York, the world's wealthiest city, with a budget running into the billions, has no educational television station and only a half-starved though competent municipal radio station.

Federal legislation to provide matching grants to aid in the construction of educational television stations passed the Senate in both the 85th and 86th Congresses but in each case died in the House. The enactment of such legislation, though it would not deal with the equally serious problem of operating costs, would be of great value.

84

The third step, one matching in importance the shift to the UHF spectrum, is the introduction of pay or subscription television. We are so accustomed to accept things as they are that we cannot realize how monstrous is our present system of financing broadcasting until we think how it would work applied to print. Suppose the only printed matter we could ever have to read were given to us free and that except for a few leaflets printed as a public service by the printers, it were all paid for by advertisers, who had the stories or articles written with a view to attracting the largest and best group of readers for their advertisements. How totally print would fail to discharge its function! Where would be the textbook, the learned journal, the serious study of economics, the new poetry, the whole rich exploring world of the mind? Yet that is the system we have allowed to control our dominant communications medium.

There were few if any feasible alternatives when television began. This is no longer true, and there are several different methods of letting a viewer pay for a broadcast that appear to be technically quite workable. It seems to me absolutely essential that the millions of persons in America who want something different from the dominant taste in broadcasting should be able to bear the expense of serving their needs. There has been vigorous opposition to this proposal from established interests in broadcasting and some of the problems raised are real and deserve careful study.

Pay television if successfully worked out and accompanied by the use of the full UHF spectrum could open up a whole new range of opportunities for educational broadcasting. For one thing, it could provide support for systematic programs of adult education that are badly needed. The audiences attracted by such programs as *Continental Classroom* and *Sunrise Semester* even at pre-dawn hours suggest the tremendous interest that exists. The inherent efficiency of television, given, as it were, a means of collecting tuition fees and a number of additional stations as outlets, could revolutionize adult education—both formal and informal —and bring a flow of riches over the air. I do not mean to suggest that it would achieve the mass audience of popular entertainment. The university professor's discussion program on current world problems will not displace Jack Paar from the networks, any more than his book on the subject will replace *Peyton Place* on the newsstand. The point is precisely that it could be available at evening listening hours *without* having to displace Mr. Paar.

If there were numerous independent stations—both educational and commercial—and if there were a way they could sell programs to viewers rather than sponsors, the way would be opened for a substantial "publishing" industry supplying taped or filmed programs for dissemination in that way. There exists already, of course, a substantial industry, largely in Hollywood, producing entertainment films in series for television use. They are, however, aimed at precisely the sort of market now served by the live or filmed network drama series, and add little if anything to the range of resources available. A market for an entirely new kind of product would be opened by stations, particularly educational stations, supported by the viewing fees of the audiences. The commercial production of such filmed or taped programs, which would respond quickly to the opportunity, could be supplemented by foundation, university and Government-produced programs. The objections to the control of networks by foundations or the Government would not be applicable to their making programs available, and the Department of Agriculture in the practical field, or the Library of Congress or the National Gallery of Art in the cultural, might well "publish" video tape as they now publish pamphlets.

Though little is lacking but the will to initiate such reforms, a realist must concede that they are at best some time away. Meanwhile, a re-examination of the basis of licensing broadcast stations

86

is in order. The monopoly of broadcasting over a given TV frequency is a very valuable piece of property, worth perhaps from one to many millions of dollars. It is awarded for three years without charge by the FCC. The only "rental" charged is a commitment by the licensee to operate the station with due regard to the public interest. When, as is usually the case, there are several applicants, their competing proposals for public service programming are considered by the FCC. There is little effort, however, to examine the successful applicant's subsequent fulfillment of his proposals, and renewal of licenses has become substantially automatic. There is no serious effort to define the "rent" to be paid the public for the use of the public property in the air waves or to collect it. Had the FCC adhered to the policy laid down in its 1946 *Blue Book* and applied it consistently to the then infant TV, we might have had a quite different development. The recently announced plans of the FCC for more extensive program monitoring are hopeful in this regard.

IX

The earlier antitrust actions of the government and the judicial decisions limiting state and city censorship powers over films have done what public policy can to free the normal play of taste and interest in improving the social role of commercially exhibited films. The National Defense Education Act, both in its purchase provisions and in its research provisions, promises to do a great deal to improve the quality and increase the use of the motion picture as an educational device. Since television has become overwhelmingly the principal means of disseminating film, the problems of the two media merge. If pay television becomes practical a large new market both for higher quality entertainment film and for educational film will have been opened. For these reasons, public policy with respect to motion pictures becomes primarily an aspect of public policy toward education and toward television.

There are serious limitations on the competence of public policy to improve the performance of the newspaper press. The economics of that industry will continue to press toward consolidation and elimination of weaker papers, and the number of cities with newspaper competition is likely to continue to decline. For this there is no ready remedy. Certainly the antitrust actions widely discussed at the time of the Commission on the Freedom of the Press would be ineffective and ill-advised. The situation is not as socially dangerous as it would have been thirty-five years ago when the newspapers had a substantial monopoly over the dissemination of news and editorial opinion. Nor is there any evidence that the newspaper monopoly towns are worse served than those with active competition among newspapers, like Boston or Los Angeles. Indeed, competition rarely takes the form of competition of editorial policy or in the provision of solid news.

I believe it is the part of wisdom to accept as inevitable the trend toward monopoly of newspaper ownership in all but the largest cities, and to attempt to offset its disadvantages in part by enlarging the distribution of information and views through other media and in part by encouraging in the press a professional sense of serving as a common carrier of news and opinion. The latter function has been aided by the wider availability of excellent syndicated columns that enable a paper, if it wishes to do so, to present a considerable spectrum of opinion other than its own.

The communications problems of magazines have been reasonably well solved insofar as they are governed by public policy, and the limitations upon a reader's being able to get what he wants are perhaps less in magazines than in most other media.

There remain a number of problems not easily within the reach of public policy, such as how to sustain the magazine of news and political comment but of minority viewpoint. A greater measure

88

of foundation support might well be commended for the "little" magazine—the literary review of limited circulation—and perhaps the more so in view of the even greater difficulty in finding an opportunity to present the works of new writers in other media.

It is of the utmost importance that the principle of low, nationally uniform postal rates for the editorial content of magazines be retained. This rate is already so regulated as to favor the magazine with little advertising, the magazine reaching into village and rural circulation, and the journals published by churches and other nonprofit groups. Future adjustments of the rate should continue that emphasis.

Finally, though an enormous range of magazines is available to the reader, it is rarely feasible for him to subscribe to more than two or three or four. Access to any considerable part of the range of informational resources in the many thousands of magazines and journals or in back issues is impractical for any individual. Magazines are almost as dependent as books on the library to achieve the full measure of their social utility, and the suggestions later made with respect to libraries will have meaning for magazines as well as for books.

X

By measures of these sorts the mass media can be helped, I believe, to present a very considerably more substantial and more diverse fare for their enormous audiences. There remain limitations, however. The range of choice simultaneously available to the seeker of information through all the mass media collectively must, under even the best of circumstances, be narrowly limited. The depth, comprehensiveness and quantity of information they can convey is necessarily restricted. For the lone user, stubbornly determined to find his own way to truth, they can be of but partial service.

To meet such a user's need, which is a fundamental need of society, we must do a radically better job of increasing the public availability of books and of journals of limited circulation.

Here again, the solution to every problem does not lie within the reach of public policy. Books certainly ought to receive the same treatment in postal rates as the editorial content of magazines, but beyond that there is probably little the federal government can do to aid the now extremely unsatisfactory distribution of books through commercial channels. The industry itself has made remarkable progress, at least quantitatively, in this direction over the last thirty years, and further slow advances are likely. However, even if the problems of commercial distribution were solved to the point that it was reasonably convenient for anyone, anywhere, to find out about and buy books of interest to him, the social problem would by no means be solved.

The great social values of books are achieved in the aggregate —in their ability to bring together the range of resources of human knowledge and ideas on any matters. To perform this service even the most opulent of private collections is inadequate. Both because it is the only present way to penetrate beyond commercial limitations and provide an adequate book service to rural areas, and because it is the only feasible way to bring to bear the unique *collective* power of print, a great strengthening of the present public support of libraries is indispensable. We can improve the offerings of the mass media, but the very quality of being able to reach a mass audience simultaneously which is their unique and indispensable virtue is also the necessary limitation on their capacity for diversity, for profundity and comprehensiveness of information, and for bringing the world to the service of the individual reader—as opposed to opening the world to the voice of the individual speaker. Their necessary and specific complement is the library.

So far the contribution of the federal government to libraries

90

has included the support of its own magnificent libraries and their services, as in cataloging or interlibrary loans; the limited appropriation of funds for a five-year period under the Federal Library Services Act to aid in the extension of libraries to hitherto unserved rural areas; and the appropriation of funds under the National Defense Education Act that can be used, among other purposes, for the purchase of books for public elementary and high school libraries in the fields of science, mathematics, and modern foreign languages. Almost the entire burden of assembling and maintaining libraries for research, for education, and for public service has been left to states and localities that have varied widely in their will and their capacity to support an adequate service.

We have seen that the consequence is that 30,000,000 or more persons have *no* library service; that as many or more have service so limited as to be nearly valueless; that three fourths of our elementary schools have no libraries; and that only the most favored high schools and colleges have libraries really adequate to support their educational objectives. Even in the cities in which we think of library service as "good" it is actually quite limited in its social impact as a means of communication. Typically only about a quarter of the population are registered borrowers and a minority of these are active users. The fraction that are very frequent users are likely to be the less active rather than the more active members of the community and much of their use is likely to be for light recreation, duplicating rather than complementing what is available through the mass media.

Nor can we console ourselves that the situation is rapidly improving. It is true that the operating expenditures of public libraries more than doubled between 1939 and 1950 and have continued to increase, but this is a measure primarily of inflation. Expenditures per person served over those years probably declined in constant dollars. Though acquisitions expenditure rose

91

from $19,000,000 to $33,000,000 between 1950 and 1956, a genuine increase, this is barely catching up, since there were fewer volumes per capita served in 1950 than in 1939. Total circulation has barely caught up with pre-war years, and is still probably behind on a per capita basis, far behind for adult circulation as distinguished from juvenile. Though the *quality* of public library use has improved, we know that in fact for few persons is it integrated with serious purposes of their lives. We know what a force in adult education the library could be, but we know too how instantly its services would collapse if indeed any considerable number of the citizens of any town in any brief period decided seriously to use the library to inform themselves on any single public issue.

Nor is the situation much better in educational libraries. It is alarming to note that even before the present and coming tidal wave of students hit, college and university libraries in 1952 had fewer volumes per student, added fewer per student, and circulated fewer per student than in pre-war years.

These figures suggest the massiveness of the new resources needed if libraries are to discharge the social responsibilities that rest upon them. I say massive in comparison with present figures, even though we are discussing figures on the order only of one or two per cent of the annual agricultural subsidy. Most of this will no doubt continue to come from state and local sources, but I think we must face the clear and inescapable need for major, continuing Federal aid to public, educational, and research libraries. The need is national, not local. It is of the essence of the communications system of the country that it is national, and misinformation or ignorance in Alabama or Wyoming or any state between imperils the country as much as ignorance in New York or Illinois. Adequate support, especially where it is most needed, is available only from national sources.

No task of statesmanship confronts the library profession more

92

demanding than working out sound formulas for such support and for greater state and local support, and I believe no measure of public policy in the whole communications field is more important.

XI

If all of the sorts of measures here suggested, and others like them, were successfully carried out, their result would be to free the communications system of some of the limitations that now stand in the way of its bearing to the individual user a more substantial, varied, and meaningful freight of information and ideas. We would perhaps have moved the individual user closer to the center of communication, so that the system would be more effectively able to serve *his* needs, rather than those of the communicator.

But improving the system's capacity to respond to individual need will not in fact improve its content unless that is what the individual demands. The richest library is of no use to the slothful mind. If western and crime drama is not only much but most of what society wants out of television, then that will continue to be most of what society gets. Whether the communications system can well serve eager and inquiring minds that want to enrich their cultural lives, broaden knowledge, seek out the truth, achieve true independence, depends on whether there are minds to demand such service.

And this in turn depends at last primarily on the educational system. Our schools and our colleges in the years to come will have more youths under their influence for longer than ever before. If they leave their formal education aware that most of the drama and music and poetry and novels that will express their generation have not yet been written, that most of the scientific knowledge that will govern their times has not yet been discovered, that most of the intellectual adventure of their lives lies ahead of them—and if they leave determined to be their own independent men, seeking out their own truths, then they will call forth a communications system that will serve them.

And if our educational system cannot do this, at least in part— if the minds it sends forth are already closed and fulfilled, numb to the unfolding adventure before them—then what the communications system can offer them perhaps doesn't really matter.